# POST-AUGUSTAN SATIRE

# Post-Augustan Satire

CHARLES CHURCHILL AND
SATIRICAL POETRY, 1750–1800

*By Thomas Lockwood*

UNIVERSITY OF WASHINGTON PRESS

*Seattle and London*

This book was published with the assistance of a grant from the Andrew W. Mellon Foundation.

*Library of Congress Cataloging in Publication Data*
Lockwood, Thomas.
    Post-Augustan satire.
    Includes bibliographical references and index.
    1.   Churchill, Charles, 1731–1764—Criticism and interpretation.   2.   Satire, English—History and criticism.   3.   English poetry—18th century—History and criticism.   I.   Title.
PR3346.C8L6        821'.6'09        78–4366
ISBN 0–295–95612–7

To my Mother
MAE HOBSON LOCKWOOD

# Acknowledgments

Parts of Chapter 6 appeared orginally in "The Augustan Author–Audience Relationship: Satiric vs. Comic Forms," ELH 36 (December 1969):648–58. Most of Chapter 7 appeared first as "On the Relationship of Satire and Poetry after Pope," in *Studies in English Literature* 14(1974):387–402. I would like to thank the editors of those journals for their permission to reprint that material here. I should also like to acknowledge a debt to the late Professor Kathleen Williams for the work of reading parts of this book at an earlier stage and offering her criticism; to Professor Donald Taylor, for his help with the Chatterton material; and to the late Professor Alan McKillop for generous answers to various odd questions, out of his limitless store of wisdom about this period. My sincere thanks most especially to Professor Ronald Paulson for a great deal of help and encouragement.

# Contents

# POST-AUGUSTAN SATIRE

# Introduction

THE CENTRAL question I have tried to answer in this book is: What happens to verse satire after Pope? There are perhaps two senses in which this question may be taken: one meaning something like "How is it different?" and the other, "What goes wrong with it?" The satirical poem is of course one of the landmark features of English literature in the period from the Restoration to the death of Pope, and one naturally wonders what later becomes of this celebrated genre that was once, in *Hudibras* or *Absalom and Achitophel* or the *Dunciad*, so convincingly alive. Hence in this book I have set forth what seem to me to be some important distinctions between the earlier and later character of verse satire during the eighteenth century, hoping in that way to shed some light on the question of what must, after all, be considered as the decline—not to say the death—of this genre. A morbid theme, then, and a book that is something in the way of an autopsy; but a theme having, as I see it, the special virtue of calling attention to certain qualities or potentialities of satire, and certain affinities between satire and other genres, which are otherwise not historically apparent.

While there are major differences between a satire by Dryden or Pope and one by Charles Churchill, the later eighteenth-century practice of satire does not, strictly speaking, represent anything new. The title I gave this book, in fact, was meant to reflect its historical stress, which is on the question of how satire in the later eighteenth century may be related to the "Augustan" satire out of which it must generally,

3

I think, be understood as developing, and of which it is indeed an extension.[1] Consequently I have devoted some of my time in each chapter of this book to the job of reviewing certain relevant aspects of the earlier tradition as a preface to the account I propose of the satire after Pope, intending by that device to emphasize the sometimes surprising degree of generic continuity throughout the century as a whole.

Much of the material upon which this book is based is unfamiliar, even to professionals, and though I should like to be able to say that this is because it has been unjustly neglected, I am afraid that the case is otherwise and that in fact much of it is not very good. I have in mind writers such as Paul Whitehead, Robert Lloyd, or T. J. Mathias, and in their cases at least I am not inclined to make any more claims than the critical tradition requires me to (which is to say very few). Still, in a study of this kind they must be introduced, if only for their illustrative value; and I can only say that I have tried to be thoughtful about this, hoping to make them interestingly illustrative without also falsifying their status as writers.

Neither is this to say that all of the material is uninteresting in itself, because there are important exceptions: most notably in Churchill, Cowper, the satirists of the *Anti–Jacobin*, and John Wolcot, the self-styled "Peter Pindar," all of whom are in one way or another talented and accomplished writers. Byron of course would also figure in here as an exception, were it not for my inability within the scope of this book to give any account of his satire, except in taking the briefest note of it as it seems particularly to have been led up to, as it were, by post–Augustan developments.

It is Churchill who is at the focus of the book. There are two reasons: he is certainly the best and most interesting poet-satirist between Pope and Byron, an always highly readable, sometimes brilliant writer who blazed the comet of a season, as Byron put it, for about four years until his death in 1764 at the age of thirty-two; and he embodies many of the older Augustan habits of satire simultaneously with new impulses, such that he stands as a particularly useful and important reference point in considering the later eighteenth-century tradition.

My preoccupation with Churchill for the purposes of this book hasn't led me to want to stop strangers in the street and pass out copies of his poems, but I do think he has been unread and undervalued to a degree, perhaps because of chronological accident as much as anything else: he writes at a time when many of the most interesting and successful literary developments are taking place in prose, or otherwise than in verse satire at least, so that a short-lived satirical poet trying to do in his time what Pope had done so much more compellingly in his, may sound hollow to us.

Churchill has Dryden's sloppiness without Dryden's genius, Pope's couplet without Pope's couplet rhetoric, and Swift's anger without Swift's conviction. So much for the worst that can be said of him. What he does have of merit is an imaginative vigor and expressive power, uneven but at times remarkable, even occasionally equal to Dryden and Pope. His overall poetic achievement is another matter, obviously —he did after all write only four years to Pope's forty—and on that score he deserves notice mainly for the peculiar clarity with which he exemplifies the course of the satiric tradition after Pope. In other words, it is possible to learn something from him about what happens to that tradition, and in turn I think to add something to our ability to rationalize the shift in idiom and sensibility between a "classical" and a "romantic" literature.

While considering what material to include in this book, I sometimes found it hard to decide whether or not a particular poem ought to be regarded as a satire. The question arises from time to time in Churchill, for instance, as also in the case of some of Cowper's poems. But it is a question presupposing a definition; and a definition of satire, or even of the verse satire, is something I felt I should try to get along without.

The most knowledgably circumspect attempts to define satire have fallen a little flat, possibly because any definition of satire must necessarily amount to a generalized description of satire as it has been intended and written and understood in the past. The more general the description, and the more satisfying it seems to be as a definition of the genre as a whole, the less good it is when it is needed most: that is, in borderline cases. I am back now to my first consideration, which was that in post–Augustan satire one comes across a number of such cases, so many in fact that the traditional integrity of the genre appears to have undergone considerable stress during this period, and is doubtfully preserved. And since that itself is one of my points about post–Augustan satire, some of the poems I introduce for discussion are those which are only doubtfully or partially to be called satires, poems which otherwise might not properly belong in a book about satire. But I would emphasize that they do belong here because it is a characteristic of satire after Pope, much more than of Renaissance or Augustan satire, to beg the question of what is satire.

In selecting material for this study, then, I have been guided by my feeling that the changing tradition of satire in the later eighteenth century would be most significantly and accurately illustrated by poems which are many of them not formal verse satires in the strict sense— few English satirical poems have been, anyway—but which do clearly reflect on the tradition. We are tracing disappearances and transformations, after all, where a definition of that which disappears will tell us only that it disappears, not where it disappears or how. Besides Churchill, I have tried therefore to take into account a representative sample of poems between 1750 and 1800 which might reasonably be identified as significantly "satiric" in the broader adjectival sense: whether in their overall conception and controlling purpose, or in important parts of them; whether in a mildly or a bitterly ridiculing vein.

The quality of generic confusion in post–Augustan satire is broadly related to the question I have already alluded to as the decline of verse satire. How is such a question to be dealt with? I think we have first to come to some understanding of what such a thing as the "decline of satire" could mean. Taken in its narrowest historical context, it means that the satire written during the last half of the eighteenth century is artistically unsatisfying compared to the satire written by Dryden and Pope; and also that the genre itself takes on an altered and diminished significance for the writers and readers of this period. And as to why such changes take place, we might consider, on the one hand, external historical causes, such as the celebrated (and immemorially unceasing) rise of the middle classes, or, on the other hand, such specifically literary influences as are perhaps most familiarly comprehended by T. S. Eliot's idea of tradition and the individual talent.

On the whole I would say the literary influences serve best to answer this question of what happens to satire after Pope. Specifically, for example, I have in mind such considerations as the large and obvious impact of Pope's example on later eighteenth-century satirists, the role of traditional generic conventions in the satire of this period, the satirist's own conception of the genre, his audience's expectations, and, of course, his individual talent. Now I do not mean to suggest that external influences play no part at all, obviously, and one has to use judgment in sorting these things out, since it is a complicated picture. For instance, (1) tastes were changing and many readers and critics had grown tired of satire, and in some respects actually hostile to it (this partly owing to extra-literary circumstances). But also, (2) the most gifted writers of the period did not write verse satire, at least not very often, or else the great verse satirists between Pope and Byron simply did not get born, or were otherwise mute and inglorious—a point that is not so silly as it may seem when one considers for example how different our idea of "Augustan satire" would have to be if Pope had caught a cold and died in 1725. And finally, (3) there is a feeling on the part of many writers throughout the later eighteenth century that their poetry is somehow worn out, inadequate to what they wish of it. So with Churchill's friend Robert Lloyd:

> Who, but a madman, would engage
> A Poet in the present age?
> Write what we will, our works bespeak us
> *Imitatores, servum Pecus.*
> Tale, Elegy, or lofty Ode,
> We travel in the beaten road.[2]

These are some examples of changes that must be considered chiefly in terms of literary genre and convention, and it is here that I have put the emphasis in this book. More particularly, I have sought to describe changes in what is (or is taken to be) conventional in such aspects of satire as its structure, subject matter, figures and descriptions, its projected author and his role, its methods of expression (as for example ironic or directly abusive), and its representation of the relationship between author and audience. The various chapters of the

book are organized around these topics. By and large I keep to chro-
nology within the chapters, beginning in each case with a fairly extensive reference to the Augustan context for that particular topic.

I hope to show in Churchill and in some of his contemporaries the
increasing self-absorption and inwardness of satire—a characteristic
linking it obviously with early nineteenth-century poetry, but at the
same time, and perhaps more interestingly, reflecting also on the nat-
uralness and, almost, the inevitability with which Augustan satire
evolves into something quite different. I have been struck especially
by how little adjustment seems to have been needed, in fact, for the
older satire to assume an entirely different character; or by how many
of the features in either the earlier or the later satire may be observed,
fading out or just manifesting themselves, in the other. This mutuality
is what I have tried to portray in each of the chapters where I set
Churchill and the satire of the last half of the century alongside the
established Augustan habits of form and content. It is this mutuality
of convention which also makes me think that at least some of the
rather spectacular differences between Augustan satire and the satire
that follows may be capable of being understood largely without re-
sorting in the first instance to explanations having to do with the political temper, the tide of taste, or the *Weltanschauung*. I stress in the
"first" instance simply because any general alteration in a literary
tradition probably has to be defined ultimately in extra-literary terms.
But such terms are also the heavy artillery of criticism, tending to ob-
literate the merely proximate influences which may have been at work
and which, when they are made apparent, will provide a different kind
of insight to literary tradition and change. Hence my interest in this
book in trying to see satire after Pope as the realization of a certain
potential in the satire before Pope—what Alan Fisher has neatly
called the "stretching" of Augustan satire.[3]

My approach, then, is limited, and has its limitations. It has meant
leaving out a great deal, such as most of the historical and biographical
circumstance associated with these satires, something I hope is forgiv-
able in light of my purpose and the fact that the subject of later eighteenth-century satire is relatively without a critical status—such that

one cannot quite ask the reader to have an interest in the topicality of the satire until he may be expected to have an interest in the satire itself.

Those who might want to read more extensively or systematically in the satire of this period will find most of the material accessible in one published form or another, although very little of it, saving Churchill, has been edited well or at all. In the majority of cases the best one can hope for is an ill-collected eighteenth- or early nineteenth-century edition of a writer's works, sometimes self-sponsored (as with T. J. Mathias and Peter Pindar), sometimes not (as with the collected editions done posthumously for Paul Whitehead and Robert Lloyd). Some of the writers are represented (usually very incompletely) in the Chalmers or Anderson anthologies.[4] There is also a sampling of this material, and only a sampling, in Sherard Vines, *Georgian Satirists* (London: Wishart & Co., 1934). My sources are indicated in the text as they arise.

There is really no established tradition of scholarship and criticism dealing in general terms with the satire of this period, needless to say, but Kenneth Hopkins' *Portraits in Satire* (London: Barrie Books, 1958) presents the important satirists largely through biographical commentary and extensive quotation. Another study worth mentioning in this connection is W. B. Carnochan's controversial, but in my opinion excellent, "Satire, Sublimity, and Sentiment: Theory and Practice in Post-Augustan Satire."[5] One of the best essays on Churchill in recent years is Morris Golden's "Sterility and Eminence in the Poetry of Charles Churchill,"[6] to which I am particularly indebted for aspects of my treatment of Churchill's self-portrayal in Chapter 2.

## CHAPTER 1

# Subject and Structure

THE SUBJECT OF a satire may include the "object" of the satire, the thing being satirized, without necessarily being limited to that: in *Absalom and Achitophel*, for example, the main object of the satire is Shaftesbury and the political position he represents, but the subject of the poem considered as a whole must be seen as also including Dryden and the position *he* represents. In *The Medal*, on the other hand, which is subtitled "A Satire against Sedition," the subject of the poem and the object of the satire—Shaftesbury, or "sedition"—are virtually one and the same thing.

It is easy enough to generalize about the subject of satire, as Juvenal was doing after a fashion when he said that his subject was *quidquid agunt homines*. That description doesn't tell us much, of course, except that satire belongs to the extremely large class of literature that deals with what people say and do in the society of each other, as opposed to the literature that deals with what they think and feel when they are alone. Still, this generalization can be of some use, as when in the later eighteenth century the satirist writes increasingly about what he himself thinks and feels, and less about what other men say and do.

The concept of the structure of satire, on the other hand, presents more difficulties. "Structure" is a very loosely used term of criticism, for one thing. The structure of a literary work may be identified with the arrangement of its parts, the pattern of its imagery, its levels of meaning, its plot, or its unexpressed basis in myth; structure can be logical, counterlogical, rhetorical, ironic, or paradoxical; it can be represented as having a great deal to do with the essential meaning of a work, or very little to do with it. For my own purposes I would limit the term to its eighteenth-century sense of "design" or "plan"—the meaning Addison has in mind, for instance, when he speaks of *Paradise Lost* as faulty in "structure" because of its having too many digressions.[1] In this sense the term refers to the writer's method of proceeding, and to the placement, subordination, and relationship of the various parts of his work.

In the eighteenth century the concept of structure is closely related to that of the subject on which a work is written. That is, the subject is seen as controlling the organization of the work. The different parts of a poem will ideally represent the different aspects of its subject, as in—to take an obvious example—the *Essay on Man*, where part relates to part and part relates to whole as Pope conceives his subject to be analyzable. This is also why we find Johnson criticizing *The Seasons* (regretfully, it is true) for its "want of method," since in the case of descriptive poems the writer is not dealing with an abstract subject and therefore has no basis for organizing his poem along systematic conceptual lines.[2]

Johnson recognizes that the structure of *The Seasons*, or lack of it, is dictated by the subject—"many appearances subsisting all at once." But there is also another respect in which the structure of poetry is considered to be a function of its subject, and that is in the simple concept of keeping to the subject. Addison's remark about the structure of *Paradise Lost* is an instance of criticism on this score, and indeed "digression" is the term one encounters most commonly whenever the question of faulty structure arises in Augustan literary criticism.

The importance of this principle varies somewhat with the type of poem being considered. In the more elevated and formal kinds of poetry, such as the epic and the formal verse essay and verse satire, the different parts of the poem are expected to contribute something to the principal subject; whereas in familiar epistles and satiric poems a certain license in digressions is understood. That license particularly applies to satire, as the etymology of the name implies.

Even in the case of the so-called formal verse satire, the Augustans pay very little critical attention to the matter of structure. Dryden is the only important exception: in the *Discourse concerning the Original and Progress of Satire* (1692/3), he says we learn from Persius that a "perfect satire" should treat the subject of only one vice. But Dryden also admits the necessity of variety in satire, suggesting that the satirist should achieve it by diversifying his treatment of the one subject.[3]

In any case, the bipartite structural pattern that Dryden recognizes as classically correct, consisting of the attack on some one vice and the inculcation of its opposite virtue, and which is described more fully in a well-known essay by Mary Claire Randolph,[4] never has much to do with Augustan satire as it actually comes to be written. Mrs. Randolph observed that the only major authors who wrote original "formal" verse satires were Pope, in the four *Moral Essays*, and Young, in *Love of Fame*. One might add to that a few lesser examples, such as James Cawthorn's ponderous "ethic epistle," *The Vanity of Human Enjoyments* (1749), but on the whole Augustan satire does not reflect any particular anxiety about keeping to one subject or conforming to a classical model of structure. This is not so surprising, in view of the satirist's old claim about the breadth of his subject, or the claim he sometimes makes to the effect that he is consumed with indignation at the viciousness and stupidity around him—since such emotional or dramatic conventions of presentation obviously do not sort with the kind of structural conventions that imply a dispassionate mind at work: "Fools rush into my Head, and so I write."

The Augustans may think of digressions in writing as a form of self-worship: the scribbler refuses to submit himself to his subject or to the aim of communicating something useful—in effect, refuses to acknowledge a necessity superior to his own momentary urge to say something irrelevant. In the "Digression in Praise of Digressions" in the *Tale of a Tub*, Swift's Grub-street Hack defends "the great modern improvement of digressions," arguing that "the Society of writers would quickly be reduced to a very inconsiderable Number, if Men were put upon making Books, with the fatal Confinement of delivering nothing beyond what is to the Purpose."[5] And yet, surely, what is "to the purpose" in the *Tale of a Tub* itself must be very broadly defined if that work is not to be considered digressive. Swift seems to supply us with such a definition of his subject in the "Apology" added to the fifth edition of the *Tale*, where he says that he had intended to deal with "the numerous and gross Corruptions in Religion and Learning."[6]

This is almost as wide a territory as Juvenal's *quidquid agunt homines*, and in giving himself so much room Swift typifies the Augustan satirist's habit of choosing abstract, generalized, or symbolic subjects within whose terms he is free to introduce a range of specific human behavior: Rochester on reasoning pride, Dryden on political corruption, Young on love of fame, Pope on Dulness, Swift on delusion, Johnson on false happiness.

In the great examples of Augustan satire, as a result, one always has the feeling that almost the whole world is proud, corrupt, dull, or deluded. The subject of the satire, whatever it is, seems exemplified to excess, swollen and stretched by the unending procession of localized cases in point. The satirist strives to represent his subject kaleidoscopically, setting it forth in all its special habits and forms; he may even try to make the job seem hopeless, as Pope is inclined to do in his later satires. The tradition of Augustan satire is also illustrated by poems whose subjects are much more specific—the lampoon on a named individual, for instance. But at either extreme is this characteristic effort to achieve completeness of representation: in the lampoon, to list every single bad quality in the man, and in a general satire like the *Dunciad,* to track down and make a public record of every imaginable manifestation of the corruption of taste and morals.

As for keeping to his subject, the Augustan satirist may very well (in terms of the psychological realities of composing a poem) move from one part of his work to another as his personal interests dictate. But he will usually never admit that, and instead will insist that all the different things he writes about do pertain to each other as elements of a complete picture. The significant point, as I hope to show, is that he refers the design of his satire to something which, like the

concept of Dulness or pride, supposedly lies outside of the satirist himself and exists independently of his having thought it up—something
which by its very generality is clearly public property.

In the satiric poems of the Augustan period one is used to seeing
patterns of common interest in the different subjects on which they are
written and feel that there is something proper in thinking of the men
who wrote what we call "Augustan satire"—Butler, Dryden, Pope,
Swift, among the most talented ones—as engaged in a group effort
against pride, irrationality, extremism, credulity, and vulgarization.

The case is different with post–Augustan satire, where one is struck
by the difficulty of making out connections between the subjects that
are of interest to the writers; where instead of a restricted number of
general subjects we have a great number of restricted, definite, much
less generalized subjects—restricted not only in scope but also in their
more complete identification with the particular poems and authors
that give them expression. For a student in search of patterns, especially if he is accustomed to the strong patterns of Augustan satire, the
effect is one of randomness and confusion.

Instead of satires on man, or Dulness, or pride, the post–Augustan
satirists more modestly confine themselves to subjects such as fashions
in oriental gardening (William Mason's *An Heroic Epistle to Sir William Chambers*), or public school education (Cowper's *Tirocinium*),
or Presbyterian hypocrisy (Burns's *Holy Willie's Prayer*). If politics
could be considered a "subject," then a great many satirical poems of
the period do at least have that interest in common; the treatment,
though, is seldom generalized but instead partisan or extremely personal, as in Chatterton's satires and, later on, in the mass of political
verse written in the early nineteenth century.

One finds also a minor preoccupation with the subject of the writer's
role in society, with emphasis on the value of his independence and
incorruptibility amid the temptations of patronage and political influence. But this subject by its very nature seeks the level of personal
declaration:

> By Him that made me, I am much more proud,
> More inly satisfied, to have a croud

Point at me as I pass, and cry,—that's He—
A poor, but honest Bard, who dares be free
Amidst Corruption, than to have a train
Of flick'ring levee slaves, to make me vain
Of things I ought to blush for . . .[7]

The most widely-read satirical poem of 1761 was Charles Churchill's *The Rosciad*, which deals with the state of contemporary acting. In 1766 it was Christopher Anstey's *New Bath Guide*, whose
subject is "local" in the literal geographical sense: it is a poem about
Bath, England, in respect of just those things that make it different
from other places. In 1784 it was *The Rolliad*, which focuses on Pitt
and his new government; in 1791, William Gifford's *The Baviad*,
against the "disease" of the Della Cruscan movement.

The point should be clear enough, that in the later eighteenth century the subject of satire is typically diminished, reduced and confined
in conception and application. And while the specific object of ridicule
stands very clearly defined in the foreground, the satirist has no special
concern with making it also seem part of some general background,
none of the Augustan habit of investing the satiric object with comprehensive meaning or symbolic significance. The post–Augustan satirist is usually more willing to be taken personally, and the thing he
is attacking may be defined more precisely with respect to himself
than in any other way.

There are few "villains" in this satire—not in the sense of those
figures like Dryden's Achitophel or Pope's Goddess of Dulness who
are made to embody some comprehensively threatening system of evil.
The characteristic tone of satire remains. But this tone frequently has
no well-defined object to attach itself to (and in turn further define);
thus it sometimes seems that we are not really even reading satire in
the usual sense of the word.

In 1761 John Armstrong, the physician and author of *The Art of
Preserving Health* (1744), published an epistle called *A Day*, addressed to John Wilkes, in which he recommends the practice of rising
early and going to bed before twelve. Toward the end of the year Churchill's poem *Night* appeared, consciously reflecting on Armstrong's
advice and the "fools" of the ordinary daylight world, the self-satisfied

keepers of "good hours." These "fools," however, are not given any clear satiric meaning, as Churchill does not appear to be using them to illustrate any thesis of social or moral disapproval. Still, he speaks of them collectively in a way that surely *sounds* like satire:

> Go on, ye fools, who talk for talking sake,
> Without distinguishing distinctions make;
> Shine forth in native folly, native pride,
> Make yourselves rules to all the world beside . . .
>
> [ll. 41–44]

The most meaningful way in which these "fools" are defined, in fact, is in relation to the satirist himself. Not that they are personal enemies—a necessary distinction here—but they might best be said to represent all the not–Churchills of the world, or simply "the world," and in that lies the basis for his disparaging condescension toward them. The crime for which he ostensibly indicts them—"prudence," or the keeping up of appearances—is a concept so vaguely conceived and casually applied in the poem as to be hardly a basis for Churchill's overbearing ridicule of those who are supposedly examples of it.

In Augustan satire, by way of contrast, the tendency is to define the satiric object or villain in relation to some agency (nature, reason, history, religion) that is independent of the satirist himself. Such definition has also the effect of amplifying the object of ridicule, making it seem, as indeed the satirist wants it to, the embodiment of some general threat upon correct values.

Later in the century, however, we sometimes find the satirist consciously rejecting the idea of independent moral values, emphasizing instead the merely personal character of value judgments. Chatterton does it frequently, as in the beginning lines of his *Epistle to the Reverend Mr. Catcott* (1769):

> What strange Infatuations rule Mankind,
> How narrow are our Prospects how confin'd
> With universal Vanity possest
> We fondly think our own Ideas best
> Our tottring Arguments are ever strong;
> We're always selfsufficient in the wrong.[8]

Chatterton is leading up to an attack on Alexander Catcott's published arguments in favor of the literal truth of the Biblical story of the Flood, and in this attack he invokes the abstract values of sense and reason and criticizes Catcott for not having more of each:

> Might we not Catcott then infer from hence,
> Your Zeal for Scripture hath devour'd your sense.[9]

Chatterton makes it seem as though he is judging Catcott by an independent, external standard, and to that extent he is consistent with the manner in which the Augustan satirists represent their judgments. At the same time, this effect seems quite out of line with the curiously self-implicating use of the first person plural in the first lines of the poem: "We fondly think our own ideas best." This is perhaps cutting it too fine, but had he written

> With universal vanity possest,
> Man fondly thinks his own ideas best;
> Whose tott'ring arguments are ever strong;
> A creature self-sufficient in the wrong . . .

the less familiar, less insinuating tone of the lines might place them more comfortably within an earlier idiom.

I have lingered over this poem of Chatterton's because I believe it illustrates a distinctive habit in post–Augustan satire. While it is true that Chatterton, like virtually every satirist, makes judgments in terms of universally accepted values, such as reason or common sense, we never find him referring his judgments consistently to any one particular value such that it might be said to be the "subject" of the work. At the same time there is his conscious skepticism as to the general validity of all judgments. (Chatterton likes to call it "opinion.") The effect of this in his satire is to throw more attention on the satirist, to make the satire seem less generalized, more definitely a question merely of his own preoccupations.

*Kew Gardens, The Whore of Babylon,* and *The Consuliad,* for example, all read as if the author were recording personal opinions about certain individuals, making no special effort to relate them or have them seem to exemplify a general subject. In *The Whore of Babylon* one man, the Dean of Bristol, is "lazy, dull, and fat," another is mind-lessly orthodox, another is a political tool, another has no conscience, another (Dr. Johnson) is dull, and another is ignorant. In this connec-tion we may remember that Chatterton in his Will said, "I have an unlucky way of railing and when the strong fit of Satyre is on me I Spare neither Friend nor Foe." [10]

This idea, that in post–Augustan satire the object of ridicule is de-fined more openly in terms of the satirist himself, would seem to refer to something on the order of lampoon. Insofar as we may be thinking of seventeenth-century lampoons, however—such as the famous ex-changes between Rochester and Sir Carr Scroope, "Poet Ninny"—there is one extremely important distinction to be made. The traditional lampoon is "personal satire" in that it is written for private reasons, or attacks a private individual; but however personal the lampoon in intentions or context, the speaking voice of the satirist within the poem is entirely impersonal and hardly ever reflexive. But the personal qual-ity in post–Augustan satire often extends to the satirist as well as to his victim: that is, he makes personal references to himself as well as to the man he is satirizing.

To take this further: the Augustan satirist sometimes introduces references to himself, but generally avoids representing any relation-ship between himself and the object of his ridicule that would have in it the fatal suggestion of equality between the two; it is a matter of maintaining an invulnerable position. But the more freely and realis-tically a satirist introduces himself into his satire—going beyond the stylized self-references that concern the satirist's indignation or temperamental reticence—the less freely he may rail and declaim judgments without it seeming to be a case of one man railing and de-claiming against other men. This inevitably happens when the tra-ditionally impersonal "voice" of the satire becomes also the voice of the satirist represented as a character within the poem.

The effect is illustrated in Horace (but not Juvenal); and in Pope (but not Dryden). And it is Pope who furnishes us with the proper lead-in to the post–Augustan examples of this effect. His later satires dwell particularly on the satirist and his relationship to his enemies, so much so at times (as in the *Epistle to Arbuthnot*, the *Epilogue to the Satires*, the Horatian poems) that this must be seen as their principal subject, the thing Pope is writing "about." He seeks not only to define what he satirizes in relation to an abstract concept, like Dulness:

> Fire in each eye, and Papers in each hand,
> They rave, recite, and madden round the land.

But he seeks also to define these would-be wits in relation to himself:

> What Walls can guard me, or what Shades can hide?
> They pierce my Thickets, thro' my Grot they glide,
> By land, by water, they renew the charge,
> They stop the Chariot, and they board the Barge.[11]

At such moments as this Pope's interest lies chiefly in representing a certain dramatic relationship between the famous writer and the hordes of people who want something from him; he is much less interested simply in ridiculing these people, the maudlin poetesses and rhyming peers, and indeed he portrays himself as long past that desire—even if ridicule would do any good. Of course this same poem also includes the traditional or "impersonal" kind of satire as well—the portraits of Atticus and Sporus, for example—in which the focus is exclusively on the object of ridicule, the satirist's interest strictly confined to displaying that object in a reprehensible light.

But this is only to say that the subject of Pope's later satires is complex. *The Dunciad* is a poem about Dulness, in which Pope ridicules a seemingly huge number of individuals, spiritual cousins of one another, who are represented as collectively illustrating the seriousness and tragic quality of the subject of Dulness. The *Epistle to Arbuthnot* is a poem about Pope and his enemies, in which the satirist introduces the same group of dunces (symbolically), but uses them in this case to define his personal situation.

After Pope, it becomes common for the satirist to write about the relationship between himself and his enemies as a means of defining his own personality and values (rather than theirs). This relationship itself, then, may be the "subject" of the satire.

Such is the case in Churchill's second poem, *The Apology* (1761), which is a reply to the unfavorable treatment his *Rosciad* had been given by the *Critical Review*. In this poem he presents himself as the "unhappy Genius" imprisoned in a "slavish state" ruled tyrannically by the makers of literary taste (ll. 71–76); throughout the piece he deliberately invites comparisons between himself and his critics in order to underline the injustice of his situation. He has everything to lose, they have nothing to gain. He is weak, they are powerful:

> Laughs not the heart, when Giants, big with pride,
> Assume the pompous port, the martial stride;
> O'er arm Herculean heave th' enormous shield,
> Vast as a weaver's beam the javelin wield;
> With the loud voice of thund'ring Jove defy,
> And dare to single combat—What?—A Fly.
>
> [ll. 1–6]

But of course this unjust relationship between himself and the reviewers only illustrates the sort of reception the world always accords youthful genius, and in that respect the poet's inferiority by established standards is virtually the proof of his freedom from those standards, not to say his genius.

In David Garrick's poem *The Sick Monkey* (1765), the imaginary author pretends to address Garrick on the occasion of his (Garrick's) return from his continental travels. It is part apologia, part beast fable, describing what various animals (friends and enemies of Garrick) have to say on the occasion. The actor speaks of himself as though he were a theatrical satirist: Garrick sees himself as a talented monkey, able to mimic satirically the characters who come to his plays, each of whom believes he is exempt from ridicule. Garrick is "sick" with the special torments of the highly publicized artist. The poem puts one in mind of the besieged Pope in *Arbuthnot*, and as in that poem, the emphasis falls mainly on how the besiegers appear from the point of view of the besieged: we hear of hopeful female playwrights,

> Who with a Play, like pistol cock'd, in hand,
>     Bid Managers to stand:
> "Deliver, Sir,
>     Your thoughts on this
> Before you stir—"
>     "—But, Madam—Miss—"

"Your answer strait;
I will not wait—"
 " 'Tis fit you know—"
"I'll hear no reason,
This very season,
 Ay or No."[12]

Two verse satires by Smollett, *Advice* (1746) and *Reproof* (1747), both showing Pope's influence, likewise focus on the question of how the satirist should conduct himself in an unreceptive, largely unworthy world—how is he to eat, how severely is he to write, how is he to react when he discovers that he has ridiculed a man for something he never did in the first place? Both poems take the form of dialogues between the poet and his friend, and Smollett employs the interlocutory device not so much to have a dramatic framework from which to issue satirical observations about the world around him, but more often as a method of defining certain qualities about the satirist. That is, his friend's questions are designed to draw him out primarily on the subject of his relationship to the world; so in that sense the subject of both poems is not "the world" but "the satirist-and-the-world," or perhaps "the satirist-versus-the world."

In itself there is nothing so surprising about this, since the traditional satiric apologia always treats essentially the same subject. But the traditional apologia is usually presented as an interruption of the satirist's normal literary activity, a pause during which he discusses himself, his writing, and his friends and enemies. It comes after his career is well established, as with Pope's *Arbuthnot* or Swift's *Verses on the Death of Dr. Swift*; or at least it comes (the precise timing being unknown) in the context of a much greater quantity of the "normal" kind of satiric writing, as with the self-references in Horace, Persius, and Juvenal. But *Advice* and *Reproof* are the only satires Smollett wrote, unless we except—stretching a point—*The Tears of Scotland*; indeed they are among his first writings of any kind. As for Churchill's *Apology*, it was his second poem, one of whose principal explicit points was that the author's career was *not* established.

Pope tells us in the Advertisement to the *Epistle to Arbuthnot* that "this Paper is a Sort of Bill of Complaint, begun many years since, and drawn up by snatches, as the several Occasions offer'd. I had no thoughts of publishing it, till. . . ." *Sprezzatura* and affected negligence, no doubt, all to be taken with a grain of salt: but even so, we must observe a distinction between the "apologetic" manner, real or pretended, with which Pope undertakes what he calls the "awkward Task" of saying something about himself, and the absence of any such manner, real or pretended, in Churchill and most other satirists after Pope. It is as though the task of writing on this subject is no longer quite so awkward.

Pope's satires project a certain image of the world, showing it to be on the whole a rotten place—such that in some of the later satires one is made to feel the pressure of this view upon the satirist himself, who talks about wishing to be left alone or ceasing to write satire. In Churchill, however, the rottenness of the world, considered at least in the broad terms of "whatever men do," is a fact that doesn't particularly require a response, except as it explains or throws into relief the poet's own attitudes and desires, which are the real subject of his satire. Pope appears to turn inward because of the world's increasing degeneracy from those idealized public standards by which he has always judged it. Churchill more often shows himself from the very beginning as concerned with protecting his individual integrity and asserting his own genius in a world that cannot care for such things. Hence the possibility, if not the inevitability, of writing the apologia before, along with, or even instead of the satire proper.

Insofar as the characteristic subject of Churchill's satire is the satirist himself, or the satirist in relation to the world, his work represents something on the order of an extended apologia (of which more in the following chapter). The same persistent, self-referential quality exists in "Peter Pindar," who writes nominally about a bewildering variety of extremely specific subjects—Benjamin West, George III, Hannah More—but who displays them only through the screen of a certain presence that "Peter" generally maintains in his poems. Within the poem itself, that is, one is made aware of the subject as the-subject-"Peter"-is-writing-about-in-this-poem.

He likes to introduce his poems with headnotes and "arguments" that have this effect. *Instructions to a Celebrated Laureat* (1787), addressed to Thomas Warton, includes the famous description of King George's visit to Whitbread's brewery; Peter's prefatory "Argument" concludes,

> Peter triumpheth—Admonisheth the Laureat—Peter croweth over the Laureat—Discovereth deep Knowledge of Kings, and Surgeons, and Men who have lost their Legs—Peter reasoneth—vaunteth—even insulteth the Laureat—Peter proclaimeth his peaceable Disposition—Praiseth Majesty, and concludeth with a Prayer for *curious* Kings.[13]

In addition to the running self-commentary of this sort of thing, his satire characteristically assimilates a great deal of self-allusion, self-dramatization, and mock-dialogue between himself and the objects of his ridicule. Consider this example from Ode 2 of *More Lyric Odes to the Royal Academicians* (1783), whose chief target was Benjamin West (as he had also been in the *Lyric Odes* for 1782):

> Still bleeding from his last year's wound,
> Which from my doughty lance he found;
> Methinks I hear the trembling Painter bawl,
> "Why dost thou persecute me, Saul?"
>
> West, let me whisper in thy ear:
>     Snug as a thief within a mill,
> From me thou hast no cause to fear,
>     To panegyric will I turn my skill;
> And if thy *picture* I am forc'd to blame,
> I'll say most *handsome* things about the *frame*.[14]

Clearly, the subject here is not Benjamin West, but Peter Pindar and Benjamin West.

The subject of Byron's *English Bards and Scotch Reviewers* is of course the current state of literature. In certain respects it is a self-consciously traditional poem, as we expect in Byron's early satire: the first lines echo Juvenal's "Semper ego auditor tantum," for instance, as for that matter the entire poem invites us to remember Pope. But Byron is not simply the "speaker" of the poem, and frequently the ostensible subject serves him as a means of representing himself more fully, even though that also involves a weakening of the invulnerable satiric position he could have were he to remain as the "speaker" only:

E'en I—least thinking of a thoughtless throng,
Just skill'd to know the right and choose the wrong,
Freed at that age when reason's shield is lost,
To fight my course through passion's countless host,
Whom every path of pleasure's flow'ry way
Has lured in turn, and all have led astray—
E'en I must raise my voice, e'en I must feel
Such scenes, such men, destroy the public weal;
Although some kind, censorious friend will say,
'What art thou better, meddling fool, than they?'
And every brother rake will smile to see
That miracle, a moralist in me.

[ll. 689–700]

If the point is clear that the subject of post–Augustan satire often is best defined with respect to the satirist himself—in which case the sheer variety of subjects must be seen as an effect of this individualization of subject—then we are in a position to consider one important change in the structure of satire during this period. This change is simply the structural expression of the change I have been describing in terms of the subject of satire—what the satirist conceives his satire to be "about."

Whereas in Augustan satire the satirist at least pretends that his subject can be defined in external terms, usually abstract ones, the post–Augustan satirist seldom makes any such pretense and in fact often dramatically renounces such considerations. This he does by means of the self-conscious digression—the digression made without any pretense about its relevance to the "subject." One thinks naturally of Byron, as when he makes his solemn, absurd pronouncement in *Don Juan*,

That is the usual method, but not mine—
    My way is to begin with the beginning;
The regularity of my design
    Forbids all wandering as the worst of sinning . . .

[canto 1, st. 7]

If the "subject" is not to be defined externally, it must be defined in terms of the satirist himself. And in that sense *he* is the subject.

That is, his personality, opinions, feelings, and reactions are the subject, as though in a diary or journal. One sign of this change is the habit
that satirists of this period have of calling attention to their satiric
responses *as responses*. Thus Churchill in *Independence* (1764) states:

> Gods, how my Soul is burnt up with disdain,
> When I see Men, whom Phoebus in his Train
> Might view with pride, lacquey the heels of those
> Whom Genius ranks amongst her greatest foes!
>
> [ll. 75–78]

And it is a particularly distinctive feature of Cowper's satire:

> In man or woman, but far most in man,
> And most of all in man that ministers
> And serves the altar, in my soul I loath
> All affection. 'Tis my perfect scorn;
> Object of my implacable disgust.[15]

One sees in such instances how close "satiric" poetry can be to "meditative" poetry, in which the poet is mainly concerned with the presentation of his feelings. With the possible exception of Churchill, Cowper
perhaps illustrates this potential compatibility most convincingly. In
the poems of the 1782 volume and in *The Task*, particularly, he
scorns what is traditionally scorned in satire—affectation, for instance.
Untraditionally, however, Cowper does not exactly heap abuse upon
these things or hold them up to scorn; what he does rather is to tell us
about *his feelings* of aversion for them.

I have made the point that the digressions in post–Augustan satire
are distinguished usually by a certain self-consciousness. Almost certainly that is because the writer who is indulging in a digression knows
he is doing something he is not supposed to do, officially speaking, and
must compensate for the disadvantage by making it clear that he
realizes what he is doing. He may protect himself further by deliberately calling into question the validity of the whole idea that the
writer should stick to the point. That is what Byron does in *Don Juan*,
most obviously, when he mocks the assumption that "wandering" is
"the worst of sinning."

But before considering Byron in this connection, it would be best to go back to some of his predecessors, particularly Churchill, who develops an equally self-conscious formula for producing digressions while also attempting to legitimize the practice. His contemporaries noticed the habit, representing it sometimes as a defect, sometimes not.

In *The Ghost* (1762–63) Churchill makes his first impressive display in this vein, and accordingly we have it as one of the main issues in the initial critical reaction to the poem. Rather typically, the author tries to disarm the critics by anticipating them:

> For instance now—this book—the GHOST—
> Methinks I hear some Critic Post
> Remark most gravely—' 'Tis first word
> Which we about the Ghost have heard.'
>
> [bk. 4, ll. 777–80]

The *Critical Review*, which was normally hostile to Churchill, referred to the book of the poem in which these lines appear as "a loose unconnected jumble of sentiments."[16] The reviewer in the *Monthly Review*, on the other hand, exposes (perhaps unknowingly) some of the more interesting implications of the poem. Focusing on the question of structure or "design," he makes the point that the poem is a "digressive, incoherent production," but also, meaning a compliment, calls it "a kind of *Tristram Shandy* in verse."[17] Finally, in the later review of Book 4, Churchill and Sterne are called "brothers." In Churchill as in Sterne, "there are a thousand moral, witty, and excellent passages scattered through this rambling performance; every part of which we have read with pleasure, without being well able to say what we were reading: —such absolute command over us, such unbounded power hath GENIUS!"[18]

Swift had spoken sarcastically of the "fatal confinement of delivering nothing beyond what is to the purpose." But Churchill adopts this view quite seriously. In *The Ghost* he ridicules his digressions but without meaning it, finally equating the principle of keeping to the point with being tedious, which in his catalogue of sins is one of the worst:

> But hold—whilst thus we play the fool,
> In bold contempt of ev'ry rule,
> Things of no consequence expressing,

*Describing* now, and now *digressing*,
To the discredit of our skill,
The main concern is standing still.

. . . . . . . . .

Our Friends themselves cannot admit
This rambling, wild, digressive Wit,
No—not those very Friends, who found
Their Credit on the self-same ground.

    Peace, my good grumbling Sir—for once,
Sunk in the solemn, formal Dunce,
This Coxcomb shall your fears beguile—
We will be dull—that you may smile.

                [ll. 59–64, 83–90]

*The Ghost* itself is the chief example of Churchill's principled contempt for the idea of writing on a certain "subject." It is after all a poem about "nothing," the Cock Lane Ghost. And in this poem, as in most of his others, the digressiveness, far from being a defect, is actually, as the writer for the *Monthly Review* would have it, a mark of imaginative strength. There are digressions in the earlier poems—*The Rosciad*, *The Apology*, and *Night*—but not until *The Ghost* do they acquire the visibility and self-consciousness we think of perhaps as "Byronic."

Here for the first time, for instance, Churchill talks openly of his habit of digressing, treating it self-deprecatingly, as though he were discussing with tolerant amusement the shortcomings of some dear friend. What may be even more important is the impression of spontaneous frankness which these self-appraisals project:

    Could I, whilst *Humour* held the Quill,
Could I *digress* with half that skill,
Could I with half that skill return,
Which we so much admire in STERNE,
Where each *Digression*, seeming vain,
And only fit to entertain,
Is found, on better recollection,
To have a just and nice Connection,
To help the whole with wond'rous art,

Whence it seems idly to depart;
Then should our readers ne'er accuse
These wild excursions of the Muse,
Ne'er backward turn dull Pages o'er
To recollect what went before . . .

[ll. 967–80]

In *Gotham* (1764) he translates the question of digression into the terms of freedom versus restraint, a recurrent moral and personal issue in Churchill:

When *loose* DIGRESSION, like a colt unbroke,
Spurning *Connection*, and her formal yoke,
Bounds thro' the forest, wanders far astray
From the known path, and loves to lose her way,
'Tis a full feast to all the mongril pack
To run the rambler down, and bring her back.

[bk. 2, ll. 205–10]

The "mongril pack" is the pack of critics to whom, as Churchill likes to say, his writings will give "employment for an age."[19]

Churchill's digressions call attention to themselves as departures from the professed "subject," as when in the midst of a lengthy digression he announces three times his intention of returning to the narrative, with the phrase "but to return," and yet never does.[20] He is also fond of the parenthetical digression, as in this passage from *Independence*, the principal "subject" of which is a comparison between noblemen and poets:

A *Lord* (nor let the honest, and the brave,
The true, Old Noble, with the Fool and Knave
Here mix his fame; curs'd be that thought of mine,
Which with a B[UTE] and F[OX] should GRAFTON join)
A *Lord* (nor here let Censure rashly call
My just contempt of some, abuse of all,
And, as of *late*, when SODOM was my theme,
Slander my purpose, and my Muse blaspheme,
Because she stops not, rapid in her song,
To make exceptions as She goes along,
Tho' well She hopes to find, another year,

A whole MINORITY exceptions here)
A mere, mere *Lord*, with nothing but the name,
Wealth all his Worth, and Title all his Fame,
Lives on another man, himself a blank,
Thankless he lives, or must some Grandsire thank,
For smuggled Honours, and ill-gotten pelf;
A *Bard* owes all to Nature, and Himself.

[ll. 57–74]

The repetition of the initial word "Lord," as if to start over with what he was going to say before he got off the subject, is characteristic, and serves to highlight the fact of the digression.

I have emphasized Churchill because he illustrates this tendency so vividly, and especially because he gives such suggestive hints about its theoretical basis: the idea that all the parts of a poem are coherent insofar as they are expressions of the poet's individual genius. But we see the tendency also in Chatterton, for example, whose satires are unapologetically digressive (to the point of seriously confusing the reader), and who reminds us of the fact from time to time:

But to return to State, from whence the Muse,
In wild digression smaller themes pursues . . .[21]

Somewhat similarly, Cowper also projects an awareness of freer structure in his hybrid didactic—satiric poems. One wonders in that connection how Pope would have taken Cowper's famous account of how he came to write *The Task*: "A lady, fond of blank verse, demanded a poem of that kind from the author, and gave him the SOFA for a subject. He obeyed; and, having much leisure, connected another subject with it; and, pursuing the train of thought to which his situation and turn of mind led him, brought forth at length, instead of the trifle which he at first intended, a serious affair—a Volume!"[22]

To relate the structure of the poem to the succession of thoughts in the poet's mind, as Cowper does here, means that the poem will consist of "satire" only as the poet has satirical thoughts. And this in fact is the case in *The Task*.

The same principle—that of organizing the poem more "realistically" around the speaker himself—would seem to apply also in the dialogue–poem *Table Talk* (1782), where Cowper gives rather more attention than Horace or Pope do to making the two conversationalists, and the course of their conversation, seem realistic. In Horace or Pope it is often simply the familiarity of the diction that is depended upon to create the necessary illusion of an actual conversation; much less often do we find them willing to put off or sacrifice a point to be made merely in favor of enhancing an illusion of actual conversation. *Table Talk*, however, gives us a strong sense of the presence of *both* speakers, and the conversation proceeds in a pattern of honest disagreement and concession. The effect is to satisfy more completely our expectations about the actual "structure" of conversation.

Even in so tradition-minded a satirist as T. J. Mathias, the author of *The Pursuits of Literature* (1794–97), there is a definite and conscious movement toward a more "realistic" structure. His extremely long, monstrously overannotated poem in four dialogues, is diffuse by any standard; the digressiveness consists mainly in the explanatory notes, which run much longer than the text itself. "Much has been observed," he says in a later edition, "as to the defect of plan in my poem." Then he defends himself:

> The Poem itself is, "A Conversation on the various subjects of Literature, in a very extended sense, as it affects public order, regulated government, and polished society. Nothing is introduced which does not tend, directly or indirectly, to that main purpose. It does not appear in the form of an Epistle, a mock-epic, or a didactic poem; but as a conversation in which subjects are discussed as they arise naturally and easily; and the notes illustrate and enforce the general and particular doctrines. There is as much method and connection, as is consistent with what I state to be my plan, or *design*, if you like that word better. There is unity in the design. Conversation has its laws, but they are pleasant, not severe restraints.[23]

And at one point in the poem itself, the author makes his adversarius say:

> 'tis plain,
> Connection, order, *method* you disdain:
> Be regular: from A to B proceed;
> I hate your zig-zag verse, and wanton heed.
>
> [dial. 4, ll. 285–88]

Upon which Mathias introduces a satirical portrait of Morosophos, "the man of method" (dial. 4, ll. 291–365).

The theme of disdain for method brings us again to Byron, whose views on this subject need no illustration. Byron's digressions, like Churchill's, are not "progressive" in the manner of Sterne—for that presupposes the ultimate importance of the narrative. Nor are they patterned on the association of ideas. They might be described simply as the vehicles of Byron's attempt always to exhaust his thinking, to express himself in completeness with respect to himself rather than with respect to a subject or purpose outside himself. The risk (or certainty) of irrelevancy is always more worth the taking than the alternative risk of leaving a thought unexpressed. Besides, the very concept of irrelevancy is a product of the Rules and has little to do with Genius, except perhaps to symbolize it—the seeming irrelevancy, properly interpreted, is again a mark of the genius at work.

*Beppo* is especially rich in conscious digressions: "To turn, —and to return; —the devil take it! / This story slips forever through my fingers . . ." (st. 63). Or take, for example, the purely personal digression in stanzas 12–14 which has to do with Byron's taste in painting, and in which we learn that the Giorgione family portrait in Manfrini's palace "is loveliest to my mind of all the show." And there is the characteristic use of the conjunction "besides" to begin stanza 36, suggesting second thoughts or an added idea, in a way it is hard to imagine Pope or Johnson using the word.

We have basically the same effect of personal amplification in virtually all of the digressive stanzas and parenthetical insertions in *Don Juan*. One notices also that Byron habitually manages the departure and return in such a way as to imply that the digression is more important than the "main concern," as in the famous sermons-and-soda-water aside in Canto 2 of *Don Juan*. Byron brings us back from that with, "The coast—I think it was the coast that I / Was just describing—Yes, it was the coast—" (st. 181).

With Byron we come to a point where it would seem most accurate to say that the basic principle of structure or "design" is the author himself, as for that matter he is the primary subject of his writing. I think it is true that as the structure of satiric poetry is made to seem "looser"—more digressive and more realistic—we get poetry that isn't completely satire as we ordinarily think of it. I have already considered Cowper as an illustration of this change, but the same point applies equally to Churchill, Byron, and most of the less celebrated satirists after Pope. During this period the satirical poet seems able to write without feeling that he must shape the entire work to a satiric purpose.

With such a shift in conception comes naturally a more direct presentation of the writer's feelings. And when his feelings are satirical in nature, and presented as such—in the way Churchill and Cowper present them, for example—the reader is encouraged to see "satire" in a somewhat different perspective. Now the emphasis falls on satire as a certain sort of *feeling*, and it consequently loses some of its identity as a genre in favor of its more modern identification as a "spirit": not a kind of poem, but an attitude, defined not so much in generic terms as in emotional ones. These changes run current with the development during the century of a powerful reaction against satire which will be considered in some detail in the following chapter. For the moment, the important point is that the identification of satire as a certain "spirit" or attitude, apart from its classical genre, means that to an extent it becomes fair game as a dubious kind of, not poetry, but emotion.

## CHAPTER 2

# The Satirist

SATIRIC LITERATURE IS "impersonal" in the sense that the satirist usually writes about something other than himself. Usually, but not always: for while the idea of satire implies that we are going to be asked to look at what the satirist looks at, and to see as ridiculous or contemptible what he sees as ridiculous or contemptible—a form of directed attention that would seem incapable of including the person telling us where to look—it nevertheless happens that satire can and does include in its view of man a view of the satirist as well.

This reflexive capacity is a well-known feature of satire, perhaps in some ways also its most intriguing feature. It appears indirectly in virtually any first person satirical poem, where we are conscious to some degree at least of a personality revealed in the tone of a speaking voice, however unrevealing in that respect the words themselves may be. And it appears directly in those great apologetic set-pieces that comprise some of the most striking and memorable moments in satire: Juvenal at the beginning of his first satire, Swift in the *Verses on the Death of Dr. Swift*, Pope in *Arbuthnot*.

What I am interested in here is not so much the persistence of this reflexive feature in some form in most satire, but rather the different degrees to which this feature may engross the character of different satires at different times. To begin with the most obviously conventionalized form of self-reflection, the satiric apologia clearly set apart as such, we have in these instances a kind of calculated pause in the usual business of satire for the sake of enabling the satirist to take up the subject of himself and to speak out directly about his own work and values. Most often the pattern is argumentative: answers, often anticipatory, to objections about satire itself, or about the particular kind of satire he writes.

The occasion of the apologia will be represented as informed by a need to reply, to explain, to justify or defend; and, as changes occur in the stock of current notions about what satire should or shouldn't be, there are corresponding changes of color and tone and argument in the apology designed in part either to satisfy these notions or, sometimes, to overwhelm them. The Roman satirists, for example, are preoccupied on these occasions by the question of whether an author serves his own best interests by writing satire. With the late seventeenth- and early eighteenth-century English satirists, the great question is whether he serves the public interest.[1]

With these considerations of the relationship between apology and context in mind, one can observe in the transition from seventeenth- to eighteenth-century satire an increasing emphasis on the character of the satirist; in the apologia and in discussions of satire generally, it becomes essential to analyze and defend satire in terms of its motivation as well as its effect or "use." The result is a revised conception of the nature of satire which by its implications threatens the presumptive moral basis of the genre.

In the Prologue to the *Satires upon the Jesuits* (1681), Oldham is principally concerned with the public effect of his satire. He is willing to present himself as an uncharitable or even malicious man in order to drive home his main point, namely, that he means after all to destroy the Jesuits, and with a passionate relish. His argument is based on the old satiric formula that calls for strong medicine to cure bad diseases. Declaring "an endless war" (1. 32) on the enemy, he says that their sins

> urge on my rank envenom'd spleen,
> And with keen satire edge my stabbing pen,
> That its each homeset thrust their blood may draw,
> Each drop of ink like *aqua fortis* gnaw.[2]

Oldham's Prologue, with its old-fashioned Jacobean stabbing and gnawing, is not a defense of satire itself but instead a defense of the

ferocity of his satire. His threatening and aggressive style represents
something of an extreme in Restoration and eighteenth-century satire,
where the satirist normally tries to dissociate himself from the idea of
revenge. Satire, that is, must be defended on the grounds that it is a
means to some purely public good; conversely, it must not appear to
be the means of relieving a merely private passion.

The argument that satire is publicly beneficial is stressed in a more
typical, though poetically wretched, example from Restoration literature, Sir Carr Scroope's *In defense of Satyr* (1680):

> ... though some it may offend,
> Nothing helps more than *Satyr*, to amend
> *Ill Manners*, or is trulier *Virtues Friend*.
> *Princes*, may Laws ordain, *Priests* gravely Preach,
> But *Poets*, most successfully will teach.
> For as a passing *Bell*, frights from his *Meat*,
> The greedy *Sick man*, that too much wou'd Eat;
> So when a *Vice*, ridiculous is made,
> Our *Neighbors* shame, keeps us from growing Bad.[3]

By claiming its power to reform, Scroope appeals to what is perhaps
the most well-worn justification of satire, an argument that has some
place, if not the first, in nearly every apologia.

"All truth is valuable," says Johnson a century later, "and satirical
criticism may be considered as useful when it rectifies error and improves judgement: he that refines the publick taste is a publick bene-
factor."[4] Underlying this statement is the traditional idea that there is
a determinable relation between art and morality, that literature has an
effect, good or bad, on behavior. Within the context of such a theory
literary values readily translate into social and moral values; and the
word "good" means much the same thing whether it is being applied
to literary works or human actions.[5]

For Dryden in the *Discourse concerning Satire*, " 'Tis an action of
virtue to make examples of vicious men. They may and ought to be up-
braided with their crimes and follies; both for their own amendment,
if they are not yet incorrigible, and for the terror of others, to hinder
them from falling into those enormities which they see are so severely
punished in the persons of others."[6] Perhaps a little self-consciously,

Dryden often likes to remind us of the way satire can serve to frighten men out of any folly or vice they may be contemplating. In the Preface to *Absalom and Achitophel*, for example, he treatens that "they who can criticize so weakly, as to imagine I have done my worst, may be convinced, at their own cost, that I can write severely with more ease than I can gently."

During the first forty years of the eighteenth century—whether because or in spite of the powerful Tory–Scriblerian example just then before the literary public, it is hard to say—one sees a hardening attitude of suspicion toward the business of writing satire for the purposes of figurative punishment. This attitude crystallizes in its strongest form around the question of motivation. It represents the extension of a line of criticism that had originated in the old reformation-of-manners excitement and had been given its most influential expression in Steele's *Tatler*, no. 242 (26 October 1710), in which the quality of "good nature" is set forth as essential to the satirist. Steele distinguishes true satire from false largely on the basis of whether the satirist's motivation is impersonal or personal, public spirited or privately malicious. What qualifies good-natured men for satire is their sensitivity to bad and good regardless of the personal context: "These men can behold vice and folly, when they injure persons to whom they are wholly unacquainted, with the same severity as others resent the ills they do to themselves." Such impartiality is "necessary to make what a man says bear any weight with those he speaks to." On the other hand, "when the sentence [of reproof] appears to arise from personal hatred or passion, it is not then made the cause of mankind but a misunderstanding between two persons . . . no man thoroughly nettled can say a thing general enough, to pass off with the air of an opinion declared, and not a passion gratified."[7]

The concept of the good-natured satirist recurs in the *Spectator* and informs much of the commentary on satire throughout the century.[8] Its more specific corollaries include several of the best known and most often repeated principles for the evaluation of satire. One is that the satirist should attack not people themselves but instead the folly and vice in people: a false humorist's ridicule, according to Addison, is "always Personal, and aimed at the Vicious Man, or the Writer; not at the

Vice, or at the Writing."[9] Another common injunction, again from Addison, is that "a Satyr should expose nothing but what is corrigible, and make a due Discrimination between those who are, and those who are not, the proper Objects of it."[10] Some critics of satire, taking this principle further, would limit the possible objects of ridicule to the sort of human foibles which inspire amusement rather than indignation.

Although these ideas are not original with Steele and Addison, as Stuart Tave has pointed out, the way in which they are emphasized creates what Professor Tave described perfectly as a "compelling necessity of explaining exhaustively one's own good nature."[11] It is no longer enough for the satirist to defend himself by citing the public value of his work; he must also prove that he is suitably motivated and qualified. Under such a view, Oldham's case, for instance, is hopeless: only consider how exactly he disqualifies himself by the terms of an anonymous hack in the *Universal Spectator*, no. 540 (10 February 1739) who invokes what had become by this late date the representative, virtually platitudinous wisdom on the subject, when he says that the satirist "should give us Testimonials of his own Prudence, before he commences Censor of the Absurdities of others; and, at the same time that he declares War with Vice, he should make it appear he is in league with Virtue."[12]

The prerogatives of the early eighteenth-century satirist, then, are considerably qualified and restricted; his range is cut down by the persistent distinction between true and false satire; and generally speaking he writes in the face of a strong trend of criticism that is at best uneasy about satire and more typically is hostile to it.[13] One point wrought upon again and again in such criticism is that satire is a weapon not to be entrusted to every writer. Here for the sake of clarity is another late-fossilized example, purely derivative, of the direction in which this criticism was to lead. The author is Fielding's old enemy John Hill, writing in *The Inspector* (1753):

> I am no enemy to raillery, when free from the stains of rancour; and think much may be said in favour of satire when it does not degenerate into scurrility. These are weapons, however, by no means to be trusted in the hands of either the weak or the malevolent: it is natural

for the one to mistake their object; and as easy for the other to pervert them to the worst purposes. The friend to mankind, when he finds himself possessed of them, will employ them in the extirpating foibles which disgrace characters otherwise amiable, or which render those troublesome who might be useful to society . . .

In such hands, a clearness of discernment, and keenness of representation, will prove of use to the world . . .[14]

Here once more everything depends on the character of the satirist, for it is impossible to asume that he is automatically qualified to judge. And in this, from Philip Francis' preface to his translation of Horace's satires (1746), we have an illustration of what was commonly thought to happen when the weapon of ridicule does fall into the wrong hands:

> There is a Kind of Satire of such Malignity, [he is thinking of Juvenal] as too surely proceeds from a Desire of gratifying a constitutional Cruelty of Temper. The Satirist does not appear like a Magistrate to give Sentence on the Vices of Mankind, but like an Executioner to slaughter the Criminal. It was the Saying of a great Man, that he, who hated Vice, hated Mankind; but certainly he does not love them as he ought, who indulges his natural Sagacity in a Discernment of their Faults, and feels an ill-natured Pleasure in exposing them to public View.[15]

The Tory satirists are decidedly conscious of this rather uncongenial atmosphere of (largely Whig-oriented) criticism. Certainly Swift has the key idea of motivation in mind when he writes on the subject of satire in *The Intelligencer*, no. 3 (1728):

> There are two Ends that Men propose in writing Satyr; one of them less noble than the other, as regarding nothing further than the private Satisfaction, and Pleasure of the Writer; but without any View towards *Personal Malice*: The other is a *publick Spirit*, prompting Men of *Genius* and Virtue, to mend the World as far as they are able.[16]

Likewise in the *Verses on the Death of Dr. Swift* he addresses himself specifically, almost with alacrity, to some of the current tests for distinguishing true satire from false:

> 'Perhaps I may allow, the Dean
> 'Had too much Satyr in his Vein;
> 'And seem'd determin'd not to starve it,

'Because no Age could more deserve it.
'Yet, Malice never was his Aim;
'He lash'd the Vice, but spar'd the Name.
'No Individual could resent,
'Where Thousands equally were meant:
'His Satyr points at no Defect,
'But what all Mortals may correct . . .

[ll. 455–64]

Pope especially admits the question of character and motive to a principal place in his season of reflection and apology (and satire) during the 1730s. It is easy enough to see why, when we consider how often he was attacked at that level. Here is one such example, where the current theoretical interest in looking at satire in terms of the psychology of the satirist is translated into practice. It is from Thomas Cooke's *The Battel of the Poets* (1729):

Behold the Bard; aghast his Eyeballs roll,
And the malignant Passion shakes his Soul;
In his tumultuous Breast a Fury reigns,
And with the fellest Venom swells his Veins . . .[17]

The noteworthy points in this are that the author highlights what Pope is supposed to be *feeling* when he writes satire and that Cooke evidently expects his readers to attach importance to this consideration.

The *Epistle to Arbuthnot* introduces the satirist with dramatic and colloquial immediacy, hounded and besieged by hopeful scribblers. In the miscellaneous reflections on himself that follow, Pope makes much of his candor and forbearance in dealing even with his harshest critics:

This dreaded Sat'rist *Dennis* will confess
Foe to his Pride, but Friend to his Distress . . .

[ll. 370–71]

His talent for writing is a kind of curse (ll. 125–34), and throughout the poem Pope returns again and again to his opening motif of the satirist as a weary and beleaguered victim of a whole range of circumstances. For the sake of Truth and Virtue only he stood off the assaults of "the dull, the proud, the wicked, and the mad" (l. 347), and as to character he was

Not Fortune's Worshipper, nor Fashion's Fool,
Not Lucre's Madman, nor Ambition's Tool,
Not proud, nor servile, be one Poet's praise
That, if he pleas'd, he pleas'd by manly ways;
That Flatt'ry, ev'n to Kings, he held a shame,
And thought a Lye in Verse or Prose the same . . .

[ll. 334–39]

Pope, like Swift, is intensely aware of that compelling need to show his conception of satire as an acceptable one. Thus in the Advertisement to Satire 1, Book 2, of the *Imitations of Horace* (1733), he declares that "to a true Satyrist nothing is so odious as a Libeller." In this version of Horace's apologia the device of the familiar dialogue puts us into seemingly direct touch with the satirist, and, as in the *Epistle to Arbuthnot*, the main interest of the discussion is not the satirist's work but instead his state of mind. When the Friend advises Pope not to write (l. 11), the reply is

Not write? but then I *think*,
And for my Soul I cannot sleep a wink.
I nod in Company, I wake at Night,
Fools rush into my Head, and so I write.

[ll. 11–14]

The shift of critical attention toward the satirist and away from his art and his audience has an effect of isolating him. The question of motivation puts the defense of satire on a personal footing, and what seems to emerge is a realization that the values and moral distinctions to which the satirist subscribes may not after all represent a collective public standard. The confident absolutism of the Tory satirist is met with a certain relativism on the part of his good-natured critic, and the popularity at this time of a moral idea like "Candour," the habit of trying to see the best in everything, indicates something of the emotional aspect of this tendency.[18]

The view that individual standards of judgment are a satisfactory and even a better substitute for collective standards—such a view as we see improving in respectability throughout the eighteenth century —will obviously bear hard against the practice of writing satire. For if, as Shaftesbury had said, a "sense of right and wrong" is "as natural to us as natural affection itself,"[19] then logically speaking what is the use of satire?

Pope and Swift also ask what is the use of satire, but not for the same reason. What they fear is that it may be too late to turn back a rolling tide of vice and folly. "In short," as Theobald puts it in *The Censor*, "we are hem'd in, and besieg'd with Villany."[20] Pope's dramatization of himself in the *Epilogue to the Satires* shows just how badly hemmed in he is. In Dialogue 1 he is bitterly mocking the current objections to satire, bidding "Adieu" to "Distinction, Satire, Warmth, and Truth" (l. 64), and concluding with an appalling vision of the triumph of Vice over everything and everyone but him:

> All, all look up, with reverential Awe,
> On Crimes that scape, or triumph o'er the Law:
> While Truth, Worth, Wisdom daily they decry—
> 'Nothing is Sacred now but Villany.'
> Yet may this Verse (if such a Verse remain)
> Show there was one who held it in disdain.
>
> [ll. 167–72]

Similarly, in Dialogue 2 he pictures himself as drawing "the last Pen for Freedom" (l. 248):

> When Truth stands trembling on the edge of Law:
> Here, Last of Britons! let your Names be read;
> Are none, none living? let me praise the Dead,
> And for that Cause which made your Fathers shine,
> Fall, by the Votes of their degen'rate Line!
>
> [ll. 249–53]

In a note to the last line of the poem, Pope says that its author is entering "a sort of Protest against that insuperable corruption and depravity of manners, which he had been so unhappy as to live to see. Could he have hoped to have amended any, he had continued those attacks; but bad men were grown so shameless and so powerful, that Ridicule was become as unsafe as it was ineffectual."

As the idea of a permanent and generally accessible standard of moral judgment comes to seem increasingly doubtful, or rather is displaced by a more interesting idea, the satirist, who will inevitably have based his ridicule on the old idea, must find himself sooner or later at war virtually with the whole world. A tone of resignation and withdrawal (as in Pope) or of ferocious pessimism (as in Swift) sets in. The world pictured by random implication in a collection like the *Poems on Affairs of State* is a place of fatuous courtiers, time-serving bishops, dim-witted poets, and the usual complement of venality, pretense, and silliness. The air is thick with name-calling, but the satires that project this atmosphere do not project any doubt as to whether these satiric likenesses will be recognized for what everybody knows them to be. It is a long way, then, from such untroubled local ridicule to Swift, projecting without hope the overthrow of an axiomatic definition of man, or to Pope, who buries the world in darkness and isn't joking. Such a desperate generalization of the object of ridicule makes ridicule or even satire scarcely seem the right name.

The Augustan satirists, writes Paul Fussell, "far from being 'representative' of the general tendencies of their time, constitute actually an intensely anachronistic and reactionary response to the eighteenth century. Their rhetorical careers conduct a more or less constant warfare with the 'official' assumptions of their age, assumptions held by most of their contemporaries."[21] The more powerful the "official" assumptions, the more desperately the satirist makes his kind of warfare, until at last he may be put in the position finally of claiming that he, not the world, is the source of the values he is battling to conserve. Certainly Pope gives some evidence of this in his later poems, where the collective public morality seems to have become a merely private memory.

## THE POST-AUGUSTAN SATIRIST: POPE TO CHURCHILL

After Pope, the display of authorial self-awareness in satirical poetry is generally much greater than it had been before. For one thing, the satirist is less likely now to observe any formal distinction between satire proper and the satiric apologia, such that his excursions into the subject of himself are not necessarily confined to set-pieces—indeed are often not even presented as excursions away from his normal or "proper" activity. He also has two possible directions to go in departing from the rather rigidly stylized authorial role that is presented in traditional satire: one is toward the quasi-tragic dramatization of himself as Pope's isolated, passionate warrior; the other, toward a more diminished, self-effacing, "realistic" presentation of himself.

This latter is the more typical development in post–Augustan satire and may be explained perhaps as the natural working-out of the extreme tension in Pope's self-dramatization between private and public points of view: that is, Pope continues to represent his point of view as universally meaningful even while picturing it as universally rejected, because of which either Pope or everybody else must be wrong. But this is an impossible position to maintain unless the poet creates some support for it, either (1) by insisting that he is specially inspired, or (2) by acknowledging that truth is relative or a matter of opinion, his own included, and that he is only exercising a right he has in common with everybody else.

Pope is inclined to make insinuations to the effect that he is inspired —"Heav'n-directed." Most of the later eighteenth-century satirists, however, consciously limit their pretensions in one way or another, almost as if Pope's role would be too embarrassing to adopt. At the same time, there is a certain overlapping in that the concept of poetic inspiration or "genius" is sometimes invoked (as in Churchill, for example) as a basis of justification. In any case, whether the satirist dramatizes himself as a tragic hero or as a man who is only no better than he should be, we find the emphasis now falling on what he is (as a man), what he thinks and feels and consists of, rather than on what he does (as a satirist).

The most complete and revealing expression of this change comes in Churchill, whose writing career began seventeen years after the death of Pope. But there are also signs of change during those intervening years. This was a time—before Churchill "blazed the comet of a season"—when one couldn't very well think of the word "satirist" without thinking first of Pope; a time that produced little of importance in the way of verse satire, unless we should want to make an exception of Johnson. And yet much of what is produced shows, if only inconclusively, that the trend in satire favors an increased preoccupation with the character of the satirist and the question of the basis upon which he may make his judgments.

This appears for example in the two satires by Smollett which I alluded to in the last chapter as an instance of the satirist's writing extensively about himself before he has ever really written any satire. The new interest in the motives of the satirist, taking in also the problem of whether he has morally any right to ridicule others, shows in Smart's poem *The Horatian Canons of Friendship* (1750), which is not really a satire but a poem about the necessity of candor (in the eighteenth-century sense) in friendship. In the course of the piece, however, Smart addresses himself to the type of the "railer," the man who is constantly criticizing others, in terms that definitely impinge on the question of the moral basis of satire:

> Blind as a poking, dirt-compelling mole,
> To all that stains thy own polluted soul,
> Yet each small failing spy'st in other men,
> Spy'st with the quickness of an eagle's ken.[22]

Here in fact is the satirist being satirized; or, more accurately perhaps, satire directed at the kind of individual temperament that is coming more and more to be attributed to the satirist.

Along with this tendency during the mid-century period we continue to find writers advancing the traditional claims of satire and presenting the more or less usual picture of the satirist as a dispenser of extra-legal forms of justice. But all this is now set firmly against the same background of incorrigibility and shamelessness that Pope had evoked in his later satires: the satirist, in other words, is as willing as ever to do what he is traditionally supposed to do, but now it is represented as ineffectual. In his satire entitled *Honour* (1747), Paul Whitehead writes:

> On then, my Muse! *Herculean* labours dare,
> And wage with Virtue's foes eternal war;
> Range thro' the Town in search of ev'ry ill,
> And cleanse th'*Augean* Stable with thy quill.
>    "But what avails the poignance of the song,
> Since all, you cry, still persevere in wrong?"[23]

The introduction of this question does not really interfere with Whitehead's portrayal of himself, after the manner of Pope, as a warrior against vice. But it does have the effect of causing him to emphasize his personal integrity (or "honour," as the poem itself is called) and his resolution as an individual to persist in making war on vice. He lacks the unreflecting confidence of older satirists in the shaming power of satire and must make a concession and a retreat in that area:

> Tho' on the Culprit's cheek no blush should glow,
> Still let me mark him to Mankind a foe:
> Strike but the deer, however slight the wound,
> It serves at least to drive him from the sound.[24]

The weak-sounding "at least" is a measure of the difficulty Whitehead is having in projecting himself in a public role. When he is reflecting on the empire of vice from a purely private point of view, he is much more self-assured:

> Guilt still is guilt, to me, in Slave or King,
> Fetter'd in Cells, or garter'd in the Ring:
> And yet behold how various the reward,
> WILD falls a Felon, WALPOLE mounts a Lord!
> The *little* Knave the Law's last tribute pays,
> While Crowns around the *great* One's chariot blaze.
> Blaze, meteors, blaze! to me is still the same
> The Cart of Justice, or the Coach of Shame.[25]

Here we are invited to see the satirist not as an intimidating figure but as a disinterested and honest man. This had been one of Pope's personal themes, of course, and Whitehead, in whom the influence of Pope's later manner regularly shows, develops it still further in his *Epistle to Dr. Thompson* (1755, written 1751). It is virtually the only theme in Churchill's satire.

## THE SELF-DEPENDENT SATIRIST:
### CHARLES CHURCHILL

Churchill, like Pope, presents himself as a solitary figure of righteous opposition, the only moral voice left in a world whose traditional values are about to be lost forever. His "subjectivism" as a satirist is in many ways a logical extension of the tendencies whose development, or conditions of development, I have suggested are apparent earlier. Now, however, the nature of the satirist's moral assumptions can no longer be so easily taken for granted. Hence it becomes important for the satirist to make his position known or even to create his position.

Churchill's canon might be divided into poems that profess to be about himself and poems that profess to be about something else but are nevertheless about himself anyway. *The Apology*, his second major poem, is one of the first kind, while *The Rosciad* is one of the second. They make up an interesting pair for several reasons. The subject of *The Rosciad* may be acting, but the purpose of the poem, according to Churchill, is to show how the author can play the part of a critic "with honest Freedom," which consists of defying "all mean and partial views."[26] And in that way not only will I play their part, he seems to say, but I will outdo them at it. With that he enters *The Rosciad* in evidence. In developing a role to play, Churchill also frames the poem —the histrionic criticism itself—within the device of his pose of the honest critic. The most significant element here is not the idea of being a critic but the idea of being honest. Churchill makes it plain that criticism is only one of any number of occupations with which a standard of honesty is traditionally incompatible. Once he is "free," Churchill can play any part, do anything better than his "partial" rivals. This motif of Churchill's freedom, his unencumbered judgment and unclouded vision, runs through all his poetry. It is the common denominator of all his poses. Freedom from prejudice without begets sincerity within: his Muse "praises, as she censures, from the Heart."

Robert Lloyd's speech in *The Rosciad* (ll. 199–226) is an exemplum of the true critic's method.

> "Genius is of no country, her pure ray
> "Spreads all abroad, as gen'ral as the day . . ."
>
> [ll. 207–8]

"Bards, to be bards must be inspired," Churchill declares in an early poem, the *Epistle to R. L. L.* (l. 20):

> Then borne on wings of fire, he quits
> The servile track of critick wits;
> Rejects the doctrines of the schools,
> And soars beyond the reach of rules;
> Leaving those laws to be obeyed
> By fools, which first by fools were made.

[ll. 29–34]

Criticism of "bards," therefore, must itself be "borne on wings of fire" before it is proper criticism. Somewhere not far behind Churchill's criticism of critics is the old and tired controversy over the Ancients and the Moderns, in which Churchill defends native English genius against the "envy" or "prejudices" that mislead the "critick herds" (*Epistle to R. L. L.*, ll. 43–45). The important thing, again, is to judge as freely as Sophocles and Shakespeare wrote. "*Reverence thyself*," had been Young's counsel in the *Conjectures on Original Composition* (1759). "That is, let not great examples or authorities browbeat thy reason into too great a diffidence of thyself; thyself so reverence as to prefer the native growth of thy own mind to the richest import from abroad; such borrowed riches make us poor."[27]

Clearly *The Rosciad* was an inconvenient vehicle for many of Churchill's pronouncements on critics; but *The Apology*, addressed as it is "to the Critical Reviewers," is closer to formal polemic and so has room for them all. Churchill is still the impartial critic, "unknowing and unknown," and he continues in the role he had created for himself in *The Rosciad*. Since the publication of that poem, the *Critical Review* had found its author (or authors, as the reviewer supposed) somewhat seriously deficient. In *The Apology*, then, the impartial critic is now the injured critic too. The reviewers do a double injustice first by establishing their reputation "by right divine" (l. 8) instead of by merit, and then by misapplying the power of that reputation in an unholy crusade, as Churchill will have it in a faintly comic metaphor, "to crush a bard just bursting from the shell" (l. 14). Before long Churchill translates his quarrel with the critics into a profounder opposition between freedom and slavery. He is an

> UNHAPPY Genius! plac'd, by partial Fate,
> With a free spirit in a slavish state;

> Where the reluctant Muse, oppress'd by kings,
> Or droops in silence, or in fetters sings.
>
> [ll. 71–74]

The critics are tyrants with absolute authority of a sort (ll. 83–101), but they cannot exercise it openly:

> Wrapp'd in mysterious secrecy they rise,
> And, as they are unknown, are safe and wise.
>
> [ll. 110–11]

Churchill makes much of the anonymity of the reviewer of *The Rosciad*, associating this with one of his favorite and most scornfully represented personifications, Prudence (l. 114). He pictures the reviewers as weak-willed types who conceal their cowardice in the collective dishonesty of a cabal:

> By int'rest join'd, th' expert confed'rates stand,
> And play the game into each other's hand.
> The vile abuse, in turn by all deny'd,
> Is bandy'd up and down from side to side:
> It flies—hey!—presto! like a jugler's ball,
> 'Till it belongs to nobody at all.
>
> [ll. 118–23]

Churchill, on the other hand, stands alone with no shield but his integrity. It is a pose he extended so far as to make an issue of putting his name prominently on the title page of the second edition of *The Rosciad* as a theatrical challenge to anyone who might want to accuse him of hiding in the shadows.

The writers for the *Critical Review*, he concludes, are no match for him, whose "free-born Muse with lib'ral spirit sings" (l. 271). "Genius" may "stoop to them who've none at all" (l. 273), but

> Ne'er will I flatter, cringe, or bend the knee
> To those who, Slaves to ALL, are Slaves to ME.
>
> [ll. 274–75]

The novel reversal by which Churchill becomes the real master of the fake tyrants builds until, at the end of the poem, Reason, "the Lord-

Chief-Justice in the Court of Man," descends *ex machina* to justify
Churchill philosophically. In the heat of the moment he lets the Lord
Chief Justice unaccountably change sex:

> To HER I bow, whose sacred power I feel;
> To HER decision make my last appeal;
> Condemned by HER, applauding worlds in vain
> Should tempt me to resume the Pen again:
> By HER absolv'd, my course I'll still pursue:
> If REASON's for me, God is for me too.
>
> [ll. 416–21]

In *The Rosciad* and *The Apology*, Churchill implies his detachment
from the run of mankind more than he actually expresses it; the particular aspect of his character which he wants most to highlight is his
honest impartiality. By the time he comes to write *Night*, however,
Churchill has taken some of the advice given him by the reviewer of
*The Apology* who told him to "attach himself to some work which
may promote the cause of Learning, rather than give way to squabbles
and literary heats. . . ."[28] The reviewer may have been Robert Lloyd,
to whom Churchill addresses *Night*. The poem itself does not exactly
advance human learning, but the squabbling is gone. In its place we
find an isolated figure brooding about the rest of the world and, most
of all, about himself. The world with which Churchill has been quar-
reling does find its way into the poem, but only as a world to be re-
nounced. The daytime marketplace in which the majority of men
conduct their affairs is opposed to the night-world where, in "Oblivion's
grateful cup," Churchill can

> drown
> The galling sneer, the supercilious frown,
> The strange reserve, the proud affected state
> Of upstart knaves grown rich and fools grown great.
>
> [ll. 85–88]

Probably too much has been made of what in this poem seems to be
Churchill's advocacy of debauched living, which in fact never assumes
the philosophical character of his self-portrait as a man belonging spir-
itually to the time and world of the night:

> LET slaves to business, bodies without soul,
> Important blanks in Nature's mighty roll,
> Solemnize nonsense in the day's broad glare,
> We NIGHT prefer, which heals or hides our care.
>
> [ll. 7–10]

Again Reason supports him, for

> No hour she blindly to the rest prefers,
> All are alike, if they're alike employ'd,
> And all are good if *virtuously* enjoy'd.
>
> [ll. 54–56]

Throughout the poem, personified Night has a paradoxical power of illuminating the reality that daylight obscures. The "shade" of Night is "honest," it is "that impartial hour" when "pomp is buried and false colors fade" (ll. 154–56). But the daylight hours are a "false medium" (l. 139) through which we see a host of dancing appearances; and during the day "pomp, wealth, and titles judgment lead astray" (l. 140).

Churchill comes to life at night, and time for reflection in those hours clarifies what otherwise cannot or will not be seen:

> Whilst vice beneath imagin'd horrors mourns,
> And conscience plants the villain's couch with thorns,
> Impatient of restraint, the active mind,
> No more by servile prejudice confin'd,
> Leaps from her seat, as wak'ned from a trance,
> And darts through Nature at a single glance.
> Then we our friends, our foes, ourselves, survey,
> And see by NIGHT what fools we are by DAY.
>
> [ll. 115–22]

The night for Churchill becomes the element in which an intensely felt independence can express and exercise itself fully. Prudence seeks daylight; Independence seeks the night. "Calm, independent, let me steal through life" (l. 188). Churchill promises to be his own physician (l. 64) and closes with a restatement of his uncompromising independence—the price of which, as "Sir Pliant" tells him (ll. 345–52), is solitude. He may be matched alone against the world, but there is merely strength, not virtue, in numbers:

CAN numbers then change Nature's stated laws?
Can numbers make the worse the better cause?
Vice must be vice, virtue be virtue still,
Tho' thousands rail at good and practise ill.

[ll. 359–62]

And he tells Lloyd,

Rather stand up assur'd with conscious pride
Alone, than err with millions on thy side.

[ll. 381–82]

Having rather ostentatiously established his pose of the independent spirit (hence impartial judge), Churchill turns to examine critically the affairs of state, in the old-fashioned, broad sense of the term. In *The Ghost*, to take one example, he wanders through a mass of London city topics: social, ecclesiastical, political, and literary—almost everything, in fact, except the Cock Lane Ghost who is the nominal subject of the poem. The bewildering shifts from one subject to another, the lightly ironic manner of introducing them, the occasional ridiculous invocations or mock–Miltonic passages, make it practically impossible to find any expressive consistency in Churchill's voice: much of the time in this odd but definitely interesting poem the problem lies simply in figuring out what is going on. One has the feeling at times that the confusion is beautifully calculated. But at other times, less intriguingly, it is obviously the confusion merely of a writer not fully in control of his purposes. In the only long section of sustained coherence, the essay on Fancy (bk. 4, ll. 289–680), Churchill's presentation of himself is appropriately fanciful and much less earnestly melodramatic than is usual with him in pieces like *The Apology*. In the lead-in to this section he has been having some fun with the coxcombs and "*grave* Fops" who must reason their way to an emotional response—those who

deign to laugh or cry
Unless they know some reason why . . .

[bk. 4, ll. 29–30]

The "upright Justicer" Reason forces us to "learn to think, and cease to feel" (bk. 4, l. 160).

Though Churchill had seriously invoked an ideal of Reason in *The Rosciad*, *The Apology*, and *Night*, Reason appears in *The Ghost* as a dangerous or at best a dull kind of value, whose more appealing and more truly reliable opposite is Fancy. This theme well suits the design—or lack of design—of the whole poem, whose various episodes are represented as "felt through" rather than thought through. We have then an extraordinary relaxation of manner throughout this poem, where the tone is necessarily pitched much lower than in those earlier exercises on the theme of his solitary and incorruptible righteousness. Churchill portrays again the type of the independent and unbought soul, but emphasizes now the spiritual and intellectual freedom flowing from such an independence, rather than the sort of moral authority which was made to seem its principal gift in those earlier poems. He is free to digress, for example, or to write about whatever he feels. Pleasure cannot wait on Judgment without turning cold (bk. 4, ll. 259–66), and "opinions should be free as air" (bk. 8, l. 251). The play of these ideas is clearest at the beginning of the long section on Fancy:

> Some few in *knowledge* find relief,
> I place my comfort in *belief*.
> Some for *Reality* may call,
> FANCY to me is All in All.
> *Imagination*, thro' the trick
> Of Doctors, often makes us sick,
> And why, let any Sophist tell,
> May it not likewise make us well?
> This I am sure, whate'er our view,
> Whatever shadows we pursue,
> For our pursuits, be what they will,
> Are little more than shadows still,
> Too swift they fly, too swift and strong,
> For man to catch, or hold them long.
> But Joys which in the FANCY live,
> Each moment to each man may give.
> True to himself, and true to ease,
> He softens Fate's severe decrees,
> And (can a Mortal wish for more?)

Creates, and makes himself new o'er,
Mocks boasted vain *Reality*,
And *Is*, whate'er he wants to Be.

[bk. 4, ll. 289–310]

Here Churchill has extended and enlarged the concept of independence philosophically, making it the natural state of a rule of Fancy, through whose medium we can actually make over the world imaginatively; and the line separating the real from the ideal grows fuzzy. But of course the power of the imagination is not always exercised intelligently. Sometimes we are made happy at the expense of deceiving ourselves; sometimes the deception is ridiculous, as when the disgusting "Whiffle" (bk. 4, ll. 485–565) is "misled by Fancy's magic spell" (bk. 4, l. 562) to imagine that the world does not take him for a vain fool. Yet such an occasion for this more or less traditional ridicule is also an occasion, quite untraditionally, for reflecting with admiration on the power of this "Mistress of each art to please" (bk. 4, l. 569):

O bow, bow All at FANCY's throne,
Whose Pow'r could make so vile an Elf,
With patience bear that thing, himself.

[bk. 4, ll. 566–68]

Churchill's attitude toward Fancy is curiously compounded. On the one hand he shows how it is the cause of a lot of foolishness; yet he won't focus satirically on the pictures of fancy-foolishness which are there for the having. He himself, indeed, falls victim (bk. 4, ll. 311–46), but with a happy result, as Fancy teaches him to shun "dull Regularity" in favor of pleasure. Now we get Churchill the mad adventurer in life, who (with Fancy's help) will

live as merry as I can,
Regardless as the fashions go,
Whether there's Reason for't, or no;
Be my employment here on earth
To give a lib'ral scope to mirth,
Life's barren vale with flow'rs t'adorn,
And pluck a rose from every thorn.

[bk. 4, ll. 268–74]

*The Ghost* itself is an example of Churchill's submission to a rule of Fancy; over and over he goes out of his way to take note of how chaotic and irrational is this poetic adventure, where he is himself like

> some unwary *Traveller*,
> Whom varied scenes of wood and lawn,
> With treacherous delight, have drawn
> Deluded from his purpos'd way . . .
>
> [bk. 2, ll. 108–11]

The role of careless relaxation Churchill plays in *The Ghost* may seem to be different from that of the impartial critic, but the concept of a thoroughgoing personal independence subsumes them both. The token of such absolute independence as Churchill claims is an absolute honesty in all the practical expressions of the self. True critical judgment thus is a matter of disentangling the mind from externally imposed rules and praising or censuring, as he likes to say, "from the heart"; so also with the heart, which when honest is free to follow the whim of feeling rather than the (unfeeling) dictates of reason. A man is not really independent if he allows his head to govern his heart, because his head is filled with prudential and interested considerations. Feelings, however, do not lie. They cut across the slow-moving "long trains of consequences" (*The Ghost*, bk. 4, l. 25) that reason dispatches and strike at the truth directly.

Most of the *Epistle to William Hogarth* is taken up with Churchill's defense of himself against a version of the antisatirical accusation of malicious motivation. In a long exchange with a personified Candour, Churchill presents himself as the raging satirist who is scarcely able to restrain "the furious ardour" (l. 58) of his indignation long enough to talk about anything else. If I had ever, he says, "turn'd misfortunes into crimes" (l. 132) or satirized someone out of jealousy, or *not* satirized someone out of a wish to flatter him—

> Had I thus sinn'd, my stubborn soul should bend
> At CANDOUR's voice, and take, as from a friend,
> The deep rebuke; Myself should be the first
> To hate myself, and stamp my Muse accurs'd.
>
> [ll. 153–56]

But of course he has never done any of those things and does not deserve any blame—he least of any—for his bitter treatment of "the gross and rank complexion of the times" (l. 180). It is a conventional defense—*difficile est saturam non scribere*—and Churchill weaves it into his attack on Hogarth so as to leave no doubt that the responsibility for his anger, and its satirical issue, lies with Hogarth and "the times," not with Charles Churchill.

In order to dramatize the fact that his satire is merely a function of its object, Churchill is careful to round out this picture of himself by showing that he is as eager to make a public record of virtues as he is to cry up vices:

> Justice with equal course bids Satire flow,
> And loves the Virtue of her greatest foe.
>
> [ll. 539–40]

The same sort of pose—that of the satirist who concerns himself not with men but only with the vice or virtue *in* men—is illustrated by these lines from *The Apology*:

> BUT if the Muse, too cruel in her mirth,
> With harsh reflexions wound the man of worth;
> If wantonly she deviate from her plan,
> And quits the Actor to expose the Man;
> Asham'd, she marks that passage with a blot,
> And hates the line where Candour was forgot.
>
> [ll. 330–35]

What is perhaps most notable in all this otherwise conventional satiric concession is the length to which Churchill goes in anticipating the usual objections to satire—such that the "positive" or honest and good-natured side of his personality is as much at the focus of attention as the "negative" or satirical side.

*The Conference, The Author* (both 1763), and *Independence* (1764) all are "about" Churchill and present him in several capacities or "offices." In each one, though, the common element is the idea of independence. *The Conference* has Churchill for the most part in the role of the political satirist who respects no party but Virtue, no interest but the good of his country, and no patron but Truth. This poem depicts an after-dinner dialogue between Churchill and a noble-man who has long since gone over to the way of the world. Churchill's host puts great stock in Prudence, which thereby gives Churchill the opportunity of expatiating on his own opposite principle of free con-duct and expression. The aristocrat's questions are painstakingly calculated to develop the proper picture of Churchill, who answers each of them creditably enough but for one interesting exception, in a sort of Mandevillian objection where the lord asks Churchill to

> Explore the dark recesses of the mind,
> In the Soul's honest volume read mankind,
> And own, in wise and simple, great and small,
> The same grand leading Principle in All.
> Whate'er we talk of wisdom to the wise,
> Of goodness to the good, of public ties
> Which to our country link, of private bands
> Which claim most dear attention at our hands,
> For Parent and for Child, for Wife and Friend,
> Our first great Mover, and our last great End,
> Is One, and, by whatever name we call
> The ruling Tyrant, SELF is All in All.
>
> [ll. 167–78]

Then are you not, like me, a slave to self-interest? Or can Nature somehow have "distinguish'd thee from all her sons beside" (l. 184)? The dramatized Churchill ducks the question, very obviously, and of-fers only the odd reply,

> Ah! what, my Lord, hath private life to do
> With things of public Nature?
>
> [ll. 213–14]

This is the one time in the poem when Churchill's straw man inter-locutor is shown as winning a round, a moment in which an otherwise purely conventionalized dialogue becomes strikingly real, its course and conclusion no longer seeming quite foregone. I would think of it as one of those instances, characteristic in Churchill, where the ques-tion under treatment is allowed to enlarge or deepen beyond the ca-pacity of the poem either to assimilate or to exclude it.

*The Author* is a review of the state of letters and learning in which Churchill wonders how literary England as he knows it could also be the land of Spenser and Shakespeare. His emphasis is almost exclusively on the freedom-versus-slavery theme. Modern writers, for example, are the slaves of everything but Truth; once upon a time poets "grac'd the Science they profess'd" and

> ... firmly stood
> The bad to punish, and reward the good ...
>
> [ll. 239–40]

But

> Ah! What are Poets now? as slavish those
> Who deal in Verse, as those who deal in Prose.
> Is there an Author, search the Kingdom round,
> In whom true worth, and real Spirit's found?
> The Slaves of Booksellers, or (doom'd by Fate
> To baser chains) vile pensioners of State ...
>
> [ll. 245–50]

As usual it is Churchill against the world, this time the world of authors who have sold their freedom to one interest or another in exchange for a little preferment or worldly show.

The result of this literary prostitution and commercialization of interest becomes clear in *Independence*, where Churchill concentrates on showing how the corrupt behavior of one scribbler, when multipled throughout Grub Street, debases poetry itself. On a history-as-decay principle the Bard nowadays is "inferior to that thing we call a Lord" (l. 26). Distinguishing between an inherited and an earned reputation, after the stock satirical pattern, Churchill conducts an assize to determine which one, bard or lord,

> lightly kicks the beam,
> And which by sinking We the Victor deem.
>
> [ll. 103–4]

The "meagre, flimsy" lord (l. 117) puts in his claim, followed by "a *Bear*" (l. 151) who turns out to be the Bruiser himself. Churchill describes his own appearance unflatteringly (ll. 180–86); but Reason, caring nothing for appearances, "look'd thro' his soul, and quite forgot his face" (l. 188). The bear, naturally, "preponderates."

Churchill goes on to outline the multitude of "dependencies" into which the Bard is likely to stumble unawares, particularly including the trap of patronage. Following an extended invocation of Independence, Churchill pictures himself as about to be silenced by what he calls "Administration":

> This melting mass of flesh She may controul
> With iron ribs, She cannot chain my Soul.
> No—to the last resolv'd her worst to bear,
> I'm still at large, and *Independent* there.
>
> [ll. 531–34]

Although Churchill does project himself in a variety of roles, they flow into each other as they are for the most part only different views of the single controlling image of his independence: whether as critic, poet, citizen, or man. And when Churchill represents himself ironically, it is in every case as the creature of some obviously dependent position, some cautious or interested view, the effect of which is of course to evoke by the contrary example the original of the value we see here in a state of corruption.

In *The Candidate*, for example, which is a bitter mock-panegyric attack on the Earl of Sandwich, Churchill describes himself as abandoning satire and invoking "Panegyrick"; having chosen the "narrow" and "unfrequented" ways of praise (ll. 203–4), he begins to cast about for a suitable object and finds Sandwich. In attaching himself to this man he admits he fought before on the wrong side; but now,

> Chang'd, I at once (can any man do less)
> Without a single blush, that change confess,
> Confess it with a manly kind of Pride,
> And quit the losing for the winning side . . .
>
> [ll. 265–68]

This of course is exactly what the nobleman in *The Conference* had told him to do before it was too late. As Churchill portrays his "conversion" in *The Candidate*, however, the "winning side" (i.e., of knaves and fools) is getting bigger and bigger every day, their numerical strength expressing the measure of their influence in the world. In accordance with that idea, developed more pointedly in *The Farewell*, Churchill represents himself as having grown weary of his single-handed struggle against these ever-fresh troops.

The self-dependence that Churchill insists on seems in his case to lead the satirist into an impossible dilemma, rhetorically and perhaps even literally—a dilemma whose distinguishing feature is a degree of doubt inconsistent with the usual practices of satire. The satirist as solitary warrior is long accustomed, for instance, to stand apart from the rest of the world or even to renounce it. But for whose benefit is he nursing along the hopeless little sparks—necessarily so portrayed—of Truth, Reason, Virtue, and Liberty? The requisite rhetorical extravagance of the last-ditch battle he envisions himself making alone against the rest of the world must exclude for example the possibility or even the mention of a possibility of reform, since in Churchill's kind of satire the question really has shifted from mending the world, or for that matter from vexing the world, to the question of surviving it intact.

Churchill indeed scarcely ever speaks of correcting or improving mankind. His appeal is invariably to one of those disembodied personified values for whose sake he says he writes, values that like Truth or Virtue seem to have no public or collective derivation. Obviously they do not derive from mankind in general, if mankind is "a rude and ruffian race, / A band of spoilers" (*The Duellist*, bk. 2, ll. 501–2), who are themselves searching for forms of Truth and Virtue in order to destroy them. One has the feeling instead that they are more properly to be located in the satirist's own mind, and that as a satirist Churchill is not so much the servant of a public consciousness of right and wrong as he is the keeper of his own integrity.

One of the distinguishing marks of Churchill's poetry, then, is what we might call his insistence on himself, in terms of which the satirist may be seen virtually as his own norm of value. Logically extended, this insistence culminates in the wonderfully apt role Churchill assigns himself in *Gotham*, where he becomes (imaginatively) king (of nowhere). The King of Gotham, like Churchill the satirist, legislates to a nation of people who do not exist; but in itself that fact is not felt to make very much difference.

## THE POST-AUGUSTAN SATIRIST: CHURCHILL TO BYRON

Churchill presents a particularly full portrait of the satirist, such that while we are asked to see him partly in the role of satirist, properly speaking, we are also asked to see him in a great many other roles that have little or nothing to do with satire. This represents a most significant expansion of the self-conscious element in Augustan satire, where it seems to me that the only important clue as to how this development is linked to Augustan satire lies in Pope's later poems. For while there is nothing in those poems that is strictly incompatible with what we should think of as the normal assumptions and idiom of Augustan satire, there is certainly a novel emphasis upon the author himself, a shifting of the focus. And in this we glimpse one relation between the Augustan satirist and the Romantic lyricist which is ordinarily very difficult to see, because of the much more obvious differences in diction and material.

Churchill also goes much further than Pope. Whereas Pope represents the author's isolation as enforced, Churchill accepts or even welcomes it and tracks down its relativistic implications. So also with Churchill's echoing, but also amplifying and making more insistent, Pope's emphasis on private moral qualities such as honesty, integrity, and independence. To put it another way, Churchill repeats and extends the self-conscious quality of Pope's later satires—the quality that has occasionally been referred to as Pope's "Romanticism."[29] And while this quality cannot reasonably be considered "central" in Pope's work as a whole, it is clearly central in Churchill's work.

One could even say the quality is institutionalized in Churchill. He is the first writer after Pope to take up a full-scale program of professionally conscious literary satire, and the first satirist after Pope to acquire anything like the amount of public attention Pope had had.

Churchill's satire, then, more than Whitehead's or Smart's or Richard Owen Cambridge's, constitutes a stage of development in which his individual management of the form must to some extent be seen as a change in the form itself—more precisely, as a change in people's understanding of the form. It is worth noticing, for example, the degree to which Churchill is identified with "Satire" in the dozens of squibs on him that came out immediately after his death.[30]

Churchill's example was an influential one, particularly during the first twenty years or so after his death.[31] At the same time, it is a superficial type of influence—compared to the influence of Pope—and consists mainly in an awareness of his reputation and career. At the end of the century, after all, Byron is writing about the glory and the nothing of his name. Yet he clearly legitimizes the enlarged and more complex role of the satirist in satire, making satire seem like a form of self-expression, and making conscious self-expression seem a much more natural thing in satire. Not that Churchill is an original influence, in the sense we mean when we are thinking of a writer who seems to have struck out a new idiom of literature or found a new level of experience. Instead he may be said to have brought certain tendencies of traditional satire to realization and propelled them forward.

The satirists after Churchill characterize themselves in a great many different ways, such that it would initially seem difficult to generalize about "the satirist" during this period. Despite the variety, however, there are certain consistent patterns. The moral values that the satirist most enthusiastically ascribes to himself, for instance, are often private rather than public: values that, like honesty, integrity, independence, and candor, define him in terms of his fidelity to himself rather than his fidelity to an externalized code, as of religion, justice, patriotism, or reason. He is also likely to represent his point of view as individually determined.

Churchill's friend Robert Lloyd, for example, writes a kind of satire that especially preoccupies itself with the integrity of the author in a venal world. Nor is he ever much concerned that we see him as a figure of any power or consequence in the world. No one trembles before his lash—quite the contrary, there is a startling sort of realism in his self-appraisals:

> You know, dear George, I'm none of those
> That condescend to write in prose;
> Inspir'd with pathos and sublime,
> I always soar—in doggrel rhyme,
> And scarce can ask you how you do,
> Without a jingling line or two.[32]

His poem *The Puff* (1762), which is a satire on the promotional gimmicks of the book trade, in the form of a dialogue between bookseller and author, is really more interesting as a dramatization of the hopeful author who wants to publish but finds he will have to compromise himself:

> Puffing, I grant, is all the mode;
> The common hackney turnpike road:
> But custom is the blockhead's guide,
> And such low arts disgust my pride.

The bookseller agrees with this in theory, but argues the practical side of it:

> You must enrich your book, indeed!
> Bare Merit never will succeed;
> Which readers are not now a-days,
> By half so apt to buy, as praise ...[33]

But he fails to convince the author, and at the end of the poem they part company with the understanding that it will be the author's fault if the book fails to sell. Lloyd knows this, of course, and seems almost to expect it.

Frequently we find him begging for some sort of retirement or escape from the world. His *Ode to Oblivion* (1762), a poem curiously confused in its point of view, shows him sometimes ridiculing "all the dearth of Modern Wit," consigning it to the "pow'rful sway" of the Goddess of Oblivion. He includes himself as one of the Goddess's own votaries, and represents himself as longing to put his own verses out of mind (he seems to realize that posterity will automatically put them out of mind):

O, sweet Forgetfulness, supreme
Rule supine o'er every theme,
O'er each sad subject, o'er each soothing strain,
Of mine, O Goddess, stretch thine awful reign!
Nor let Mem'ry steal one note,
Which this rude hand to Thee hath wrote!
So shalt thou save me from the Poet's shame,
Tho' on the letter'd Rubric Dodsley post my Name.[34]

It might be possible to interpret this simply as ironic ventriloquism of some sort—Lloyd pretending to be a "Modern"—except that the same speaker also attacks, quite unironically, the modern poets of "warbled woe" or "tinkling bell." So it would seem that the satirist in this case seeks a retreat not only from the world but even from himself.

In this connection the conclusion of his *Familiar Epistle to J. B. Esq.* (1762) should be considered, as it projects a similar feeling of contempt for the world in which he finds himself, characteristically intermingled with a certain determined sense of his own inferiority:

—Oh! had it pleas'd my wiser betters
That I had never tasted letters,
Then no Parnassian maggots bred,
Like fancies in a madman's head,
No graspings at an idle name,
No childish hope of future fame,
No impotence of wit had ta'en
Possession of my muse-struck brain.

This sounds something like Pope in *Arbuthnot*, except that Pope would never have characterized himself as having been possessed by an "impotence of wit." So also with the final lines, in which Lloyd, like Pope, longs for retirement, but for different (and sadder) reasons:

—O! for a pittance of my own,
That I might live unsought, unknown!
Retir'd from all this pedant strife,
Far fom the cares of bust'ling life;
Far from the wits, the fools, the great,
And all the little world I hate.[35]

Chatterton as a satirist also appears in a rejected or uncompromising-
ly personal role, unable to make terms with the world. He is fond of
comparing his situation to Richard Savage's, who like Chatterton had
been unable to find proper nourishment in the brutal commercial
values of Bristol:

> But bred in Bristol's mercenary Cell,
> Compell'd in Scenes of Avarice to dwell,
> What gen'rous Passion can my dross refine?
> What besides Interest can direct the line?
> And should a galling truth like this be told,
> By me, instructed here to slave for Gold,
> My prudent Neighbors (who can read) would see,
> Another Savage to be starv'd in me.[36]

This is satire, certainly, but the thing being satirized is really only a
background against which we are asked to see the author himself.
There is a similar effect in the following passage from the same poem,
where Chatterton makes certain satiric thrusts at the means by which
other poets achieve popularity—this not so much for the sake of
satirizing them as to assert his own position *apart* from them:

> Alas! I was not born beyond the Tweed.
> To public favour I have no pretence,
> If public favour is the Child of Sense:
> To paraphrase on Home in Armstrongs Rhimes;
> To decorate Fingal in sounding Chimes;
> The self sufficient Muse was never known,
> But shines in trifling Dullness all her own.[37]

In Christopher Anstey's satire the author is characteristically withdrawn from the work, and instead of declamation in the first person
we have satire by means of verse letters to and from various characters.
For that reason there is little in the way of direct personal allusion. But
Anstey does sometimes provide what amounts to the same thing, in the
form of an occasional dramatic "scene" involving the author as a character. At the end of the *New Bath Guide* (1766), the ghost of James
Quin is made to appear to the author of the Guide, and their conversation comprises the author's apology for the work. In this dialogue

Anstey appears as an unassuming country squire-turned-writer who is mainly concerned with the question of the decency and good intentions of his satire.

> But perish my voice, and untun'd be my lyre,
> If my verse one indelicate thought shall inspire . . .

May the river flood his hay-fields, "may my dogs never hunt":

> Such ills be my portion, and others much worse,
> If slander or calumny poison my verse,
> If ever my well-behav'd Muse shall appear
> *Indecently droll,* unpolitely severe.[38]

The "Appendix" to Anstey's burlesque epistle *The Patriot* (1767) dramatizes a scene in the shop of the author's bookseller, in the course of which the author overhears the inane and wrong-headed comments of some of the customers on *The Patriot.* We hear him once in an aside:

> Racks! tortures! damnation! death! hell! and confusion!
> They have no kind of taste for a classic allusion!

Throughout the scene the author is represented as having to put up with a tasteless and sensation-seeking world of booksellers and book-buyers. The happily cynical bookseller tells him his satire isn't libellous enough:

> 'Tis your daggering stuff, my good friend, you will find,
> That hits the malevolent taste of mankind.

And when he offers him six pounds for his copyright and throws in an invitation to a "family dinner," as he calls it, with a group of his hacks, the author disdains the offer and bids him goodbye. We last see him licking his wounds at the Black Bull—"I am laughed at by women, and vile poetasters"—and finally deciding to give up "the paths of ambition" for purely intellectual pleasures.

The poem is particularly revealing in the extent to which the author himself is satirized for his illusions and vanity. At the beginning of the scene in the bookshop the author enters "smiling and rubbing his Hands," quite absurdly confident that his book has been sold out and the bookseller will need more copies. But later, when the bookseller points to the unpacked books in the corner, the marginal direction tells us that "author turns pale." And when the bookseller notices this and asks him if he is "a little dejected," he bites his lips and insists, "Not at all—not at all—I'm surpriz'd you suspect it!" [39]

Anstey's satirist, unlike Churchill's, has no heroic pretensions, and when his small vanities are exposed in this way it seems quite in keeping with the overall context of good humor that characterizes Anstey's satire. Even when the satirist is his more traditionally heroic self, however, as in the handful of satires by William Mason, he may still expose himself in an unflatteringly realistic manner not to be found in Augustan satire. Mason's *Heroic Epistle to Sir William Chambers*, ironically and at times brilliantly attacking Chambers' book on oriental gardening, came out anonymously in 1773 and went through seven editions in that year alone. The pieces that followed show an increasing self-consciousness, in direct response to the popularity of the first poem and the public curiosity about the identity of its author. It is one of the most clear-cut cases in the period of a satirist's writing more about himself as he becomes a subject of greater public interest.

Self-allusion in the *Heroic Epistle* is kept at a minimum, and what there is is ironic. But his next poem, the *Heroic Postscript to the Public* (1774), begins:

> I that of late, Sir William's Bard, and Squire,
> March'd with his helm and buckler on my lyre,
>
> . . . . . . . . . . . . . .
>
> Now to the Public tune my grateful lays,
> Warm'd with the sun-shine of the Public praise . . .

He quotes some words of praise from one of the reviews, and, taking the cue from the public, sets himself up as a force to be reckoned with:

> For now, my Muse, thy fame is fixt as fate,
> Tremble, ye Fools I scorn, ye Knaves I hate . . .

The satirist has "arrived," and what is more, is writing about his arrival. He promises more serious stuff in the future, if his country claims "a graver strain" from him: satires against "hireling peers" or corrupt M.P.'s, for instance. The poem ends threateningly:

> Yes, ye faithless crew,
> His Muse's vengeance shall your crimes pursue,
> Stretch you on satire's rack, and bid you lie
> Fit garbage for the hell-hound, Infamy.[40]

In his next poem, the *Ode to Mr. Pinchbeck* (1776), Mason establishes his pseudonymous author "Malcolm McGreggor." And in the following year, the satirist once more takes up the subject of himself in the *Epistle to Dr. Shebbeare*. This time, however, he is chastened, and willingly reveals himself in a somewhat foolish position:

> In me the nation plac'd its tuneful hope,
> Its second Churchill, or at least its Pope:
> Proudly I prick'd along, Sir William's squire,
> Bade kings recite my strains, and queens admire;
> Chaste maids of honour prais'd my stout endeavour,
> Sir Thomas swore 'The fellow was damn'd clever.'
> But popularity, alas! has wings,
> And flits as soon from poets as from Kings.
> My pompous Postscript found itself disdain'd
> As much as Milton's Paradise regain'd—
> And when I dar'd the Patent Snuffers handle,
> To trim with Pinchy's aid, Old England's candle,
> The lyric muse, so lame was her condition,
> Could hardly hop beyond a fifth edition.[41]

The point here is that this self-review is a realistic one, not especially stylized. It reduces rather than improves the speaker's rhetorical position as a satirist, and thus it must be seen mainly in terms of its effectiveness as self-expression; as that, it *is* effective, no doubt on account of the very tone of self-deprecation that makes it ineffective in enhancing Mason's role as a powerful satirist. (At the same time, I should note that the rest of the poem contains some of Mason's most effective satire.)

This effect of self-deprecation is something that occurs occasionally in Churchill, but it is not until the end of the century that satirists begin to seek and sustain it deliberately. It is one of the most distinctive features of Peter Pindar's satire, for example:

> Why am I persecuted for my Rhymes,
> That *kindly* try to *cobble* Kings and Times?
> To mine, Charles Churchill's rage was downright rancour.
> *He* was a first-rate Man of War to *me*,
> Thundering amidst a high tempestuous sea:
> I'm a small Cockboat bobbing at an anchor;
> Playing with Patereroes, that alarm,
> Yet scorn to do a bit of harm.[42]

By the more or less official literary standards of the time, Peter Pindar is a hopelessly "low" writer. Mathias calls him "the scorn of every man of character and of virtue."[43] And certainly, regardless of his superb (and rather unfortunately neglected) talents in the way of burlesque humor, he is not in the "high" line of satire running from Dryden through Pope and Churchill to William Gifford. But although he must be linked in many ways with the mainly anonymous, unself-conscious tradition of state poems, satiric ballads, and political squibs, he has all the engaging self-awareness, and more, of a Pope or Churchill. "Peter" is his perennial, all-engrossing subject, the unvarying term of reference common to all his poems.

In contrast to Pope, however, the treatment is entirely comic. Whereas Pope makes mock heroes of other people, Peter is frequently his own mock hero, especially in the headnotes with which he often introduces his poems. The "Argument" of *Peter's Prophecy* (1788), for instance, begins as follows: "A sublime and poetical Exordium, in which the Bard applaudeth himself, condemneth his Sovereign, and condescendeth to instruct Sir Joseph Banks, F.R.S."[44] Such is the comically inflated running commentary that constitutes one particularly distinctive feature of Peter's writing. Or this from *An Ode to My Ass, Peter* (1791):

> I say, O Peter! *little* didst thou *think*,
> That *I*, thy Namesake, in immortal ink
> Should dip my pen, and rise a *wondrous Bard*;
> And gain such Praise, Sublimity's reward . . .[45]

In Peter's hands, then, the satirist is a clownish and self-parodic figure, serving principally to engage the reader in the comic effect and incidentally to protect Peter, who knows he is considered "low," from being considered a fool to boot. He is constantly seeking to disarm the opposition by such maneuvers as breaking off in the middle of a piece, pretending to hear some objection from one of his readers, answering it, and moving on. His dialogue–satire *One Thousand Seven Hundred and Ninety-Six* shows the traditional Juvenalian satirist "contained" as a character in the dialogue, himself and his attitudes the subject of inquiry and even ridicule. Juvenalian seriousness, for Peter at least, is simply beyond the realm of possibility. But it can serve for a joke, as in the preface to *A Rowland for an Oliver* (1790): "In the fulness of my passion, I at first set me down and said to myself, *Facit indignatio versus*; when, behold! in less than two hours I knocked off the following poem."[46]

This is only to say that for *some* satirists, like Peter, the Juvenalian pose is a little embarrassing. Yet this is also the same period of time—the 1790s—during which the so-called "Juvenalian revival" is at its height.[47] The revival manifests itself in satirists who adopt the manner, or what they think to be the manner, of Juvenal, as well as in imitations, paraphrases, new translations, and criticism. Simply his name takes on popular significance, as we see it surfacing from time to time in the minor material as a pseudonym: "Paul Juvenal," or even (of all things) "Horace Juvenal."[48] The leading light in all this is of course Gifford, whose editorship of the *Anti–Jacobin* and translation of Juvenal in 1802 may be taken as the high points of this phenomenon.

In view of the picture I have been developing of the satirist as a diminished and more freely personal figure in the poem, it would be proper here to reflect briefly on the relationship between this and the Juvenalian tendency. These represent those two different directions in which, as I have already indicated, the post–Augustan representations of the satirist seem chiefly to move—one toward ironic self-portrayal and the character of the satirist-satirized, the other toward self-glorification and the satirist–hero. In either case, however, there is an expansion of the authorial role in the poem, a distinctively self-conscious quality, and an implied or declared feeling on the part of the speaker that he is apart and unto himself.

The interest in Juvenal at the end of the century is manneristic, as is usual with a "revival." W. B. Carnochan describes how Juvenal during this period is made over in a specifically post–Augustan, anti–Augustan image: admired for his poetic ardor, his sublimity, his sentiment and passion, and, one might risk adding, the spontaneous overflowing of his powerful feeling.[49] Obviously, given the historical moment, these are qualities we should expect to find liked and exaggerated in Juvenal.

The fact that the emphasis falls so on Juvenal's personality as it is thought to be reflected in his satire brings the Juvenalian revival somewhat into line with the subject of the post–Augustan satirist as I have been treating it. The connection between the satirist-satirized and the satirist-hero, the ironical "diminishing" and the lyrical "enlarging" of the satirist, is really after all very close. In both cases the satirist insists upon the inefficacy of satire (Lloyd and Gifford, the one anxious and unsure, the other arrogant and self-righteous, both make a major point of this). And in both cases the satirist displays, ironically or comically or melodramatically, an absorbing awareness of his own inefficacy and isolation. One particularly good illustration of the connection is in the *Anti–Jacobin* satire. Here, because of the collective and anonymous authorship, the question of the role of the satirist would seem to be a tricky one. But what we have in *New Morality* (1798), the curtain-piece of the series, is a *search* for a satirist. The spirit of the search is "Juvenalian," of course, and the satirist they are looking for is a "Juvenal," but there is no one forthcoming. He may simply be too lazy:

> Bethink thee, Gifford; when some future age
> Shall trace the promise of thy playful page;—
> "The hand which brush'd a swarm of fools away,
> "Should rouse to grasp a more reluctant prey!"—
> Think then, will pleaded indolence excuse
> The tame secession of thy languid Muse?
>
> Ah! where is now that promise? why so long
> Sleep the keen shafts of satire and of song?
> Oh! come with Taste and Virtue at thy side,
> With ardent zeal inflamed, and patriot pride;
> With keen poetic glance direct the blow,
> And empty all thy quiver on the foe:

No pause—no rest—till weltering on the ground
The poisonous hydra lies, and pierced with many a wound.[50]

Following a rather more qualified appeal to T. J. Mathias comes the thought that

Yet more remain unknown: for who can tell
What bashful genius, in some rural cell,
As year to year, and day succeeds to day,
In joyless leisure wastes his life away?
In him the flame of early fancy shone;
His genuine worth his old companions own;
In childhood and in youth their chief confess'd,
His master's pride his pattern to the rest.
Now far aloof retiring from the strife
Of busy talents and of active life,
As, from the loop-holes of retreat, he views
Our stage, verse, pamphlets, politics, and news,
He loathes the world,—or, with reflection sad,
Concludes it irrecoverably mad;
Of taste, of learning, morals, all bereft,
No hope, no prospect to redeem it left.

[ll. 55–70]

This is generally what satirists had been portraying themselves as feeling for some time. It is perhaps a measure of the strength of the subjectivist, world-renouncing tendency in satire to find it here made a definite fact to be taken into account and acted upon.

The rest of the poem *is* a satire, of course, on the various manifestations of "the *New Philosophy* of modern times" (l. 86). But each fresh object of attack is introduced by announcing something to the effect of "here is another thing for which we need a satirist," as "Justice!—here, Satire, strike! 'twere sin to spare!" (l. 159). In other words, this is satire framed by the general question, What has happened to Satire? And the figurative proposition upon which the poem operates is that its true author, the satirist–hero, has run away from the job of writing it.

Byron, as it happens, also issues a call in *English Bards and Scotch Reviewers* for "some genuine bard" to rouse up and "drive this pestilence from out the land" (ll. 687–88), just as in *Don Juan* he says he "wants a hero." But Byron clearly understands that the role of the satirist–hero is one that must be left unfilled, that its meaning is mainly historical: once there was Pope, once there was Gifford, but what now? What we are given instead is the substitute figure of Byron himself, who very carefully keeps away from anything resembling a heroic role:

> I have brought this world about my ears, and eke
>     The other; that's to say, the Clergy—who
> Upon my head have bid their thunders break
>     In pious libels by no means a few.
> And yet I can't help scribbling once a week,
>     Tiring old readers, nor discovering new.
> In Youth I wrote because my mind was full,
> And *now* because I feel it growing dull.
>
> [*Don Juan*, canto 14, st. 10]

Byron's presentation of himself is a subject that takes us further into the special qualities of Romantic poetry and thought than it is possible to go here. For that matter, I am afraid it would be straining a thesis to apply the concept of the role of the satirist to Byron, since his "role" as a speaker or narrator takes in so much more than satire. To some extent, of course, the same thing may be said of Pope and Churchill. But in their case it seems as though the satiric role is being made to expand, while in Byron the expansion has already taken place and he assumes at the outset a comprehensively personal role that includes Byron-the-satirist, certainly, but only as one aspect (he would insist!) of Byron-the-man.

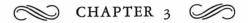

CHAPTER 3

# Personified Abstractions

## TWO TRADITIONS

THE DEVICE OF personification, which was in Dryden and Pope a customary, but by no means overworked, figure of expression, in Churhill's poetry amounts almost to a rhetorical fixation. Whole passages of his poems are thick with the names of abstractions brought more or less to life by a syntactic imputation or, sometimes, by a full-scale descriptive treatment. The habit is one he shares not so much with his predecessors in the tradition of satirical poetry as with certain poets of the middle years of the century—Collins, Gray, even Johnson, in a different way—poets in whom the device seems much more important and needful than it seems in Dryden or Pope.

Churchill's fondness for this form of expression illustrates a melding of two basically different traditions of poetical usage, and for that matter of two basically different ideas about language. His example is important because one sees in it what I would call a characteristic post–Augustan accommodation of these two traditions. The first of these traditions may be associated with Locke's theory of language and is exemplified particularly in much seventeenth- and eighteenth-century satirical poetry. Here are two examples, the first from Dryden, the second from Pope:

> But wild Ambition loves to slide, not stand,
> And Fortune's ice prefers to Virtue's land.[1]

73

Let Envy howl while Heav'n's whole Chorus sings,
And bark at Honour not confer'd by Kings;
Let Flatt'ry sickening see the Incense rise,
Sweet to the World, and grateful to the Skies . . .[2]

Chester F. Chapin some years ago distinguished two types of personification he termed "allegorical" and "metaphorical": "The metaphorical type is especially suited to the purposes of the neoclassic 'poetry of statement,' while the allegorical type is especially favored by those mid-century poets who derive much of their inspiration from the minor poems of Milton."[3] My examples from Dryden and Pope will illustrate the type of the purely rhetorical or "metaphorical" personification, where the abstractions being personified have an expressive rather than a thematic function: their purpose is chiefly to communicate a meaning which preserves concrete or dramatic force with the comprehension of general statement, creating an effect which in its enlargement of context and its economy resembles metaphor.[4]

The extreme instance of this tradition of rhetorical or "metaphorical" personification would seem to be Johnson: "Till Declamation roar'd, while Passion slept." Within this tradition, and for Dryden, Pope, or Johnson, the abstraction personified is not often of particular interest in itself. It serves a purpose of poetical expression, of course, but cannot serve, say, as the subject of the poem, or as the object of the poet's attention. It is after all only the name of an idea—a general idea, which by its very generality is public property. The poet calls upon it not to give us an interpretation of it—none is needed—but rather to take a shortcut in communicating meaning, by trading upon the large commonality of understanding which such ideas represent.

No one more characteristically than Johnson insists on keeping straight the relationship between thing, idea, and word: in the Preface to the *Dictionary*, he says he is "not yet so lost in lexicography, as to forget that *words are the daughters of earth, and that things are the sons of heaven.* Language is only the instrument of science, and words are but the signs of ideas."[5] The emphasis on these distinctions goes back particularly to Locke; their predicate is a practical view of language as an ideally transparent medium of communication between men in society: "I may at least say," Locke writes in the *Essay Concern-*

*ing Human Understanding*, " that we should have a great many fewer disputes in the world, if words were taken for what they are, the signs of our ideas only; and not for things themselves." [6] Over and over he insists that words "stand for nothing but *the ideas in the mind of him that uses them*, how imperfectly soever or carelessly those ideas are collected from the things which they are supposed to represent" (bk. 3, chap. 2, para. 2). They do not *"stand also for the reality of things"* (bk. 3, chap. 2, para. 5).

In the *Enquiry into the Sublime and Beautiful*, Burke rejects the belief that words directly raise images in the mind. "Indeed it is impossible," he says, "in the rapidity and quick succession of words in conversation, to have ideas both of the sound of the word, and of the thing represented." [7] Later, in an aside on the possibility that the names of colors create the colors in the mind, he writes: "I know very well that the mind possesses a faculty of raising such images at pleasure; but then an act of the will is necessary to this; and in ordinary conversation or reading it is very rarely that any image at all is excited in the mind." And finally, "it is not only of those ideas which are commonly called abstract, and of which no image at all *can* be formed, but even of particular real beings, that we converse without having any idea of them excited in the imagination; as will certainly appear on a diligent examination of our own minds" (pt. 5, sect. 4).

Burke's discussion of words is, in 1757, defensive. From Addison's essay series on the pleasures of the imagination, where we hear that words can have "so great a force in them that a description often gives us more lively ideas than the sight of things themselves," [8] to Joseph Warton's statement that "the use, the force, and the excellence of language, certainly consists in raising *clear, complete*, and *circumstantial* images, and in turning *readers* into *spectators*," [9] there is in criticism and critical theory an unmistakably rising emphasis on imagery or "description" in poetry, even as the essence of poetry. It is an emphasis usually justified, as Addison and Warton justify it, by reference to the power words supposedly have of raising images in the mind, of turning readers into spectators.

Such an idea about the visual power of words implies a view of language very different from the one Locke had taken—a more nearly

Romantic or Platonic view, probably, but in any event a view in which the word itself may be something more than the conventionalized sign of an idea. It may indeed, despite Locke, virtually stand also for the reality of the thing.

Burke, after Locke, would deny that an image can be given to an abstract idea. But of course that is exactly what a number of poets at midcentury were trying to do. Their models were not Dryden or Pope but Spenser and Milton, in whose tradition the device of personification regularly involves an allegorical depiction of the abstract idea. If it is important to turn the reader of poetry into a spectator, then the poet who invokes an abstraction will naturally tend to make an imaginary picture of it. Joseph Warton in the *Ode to Fancy* (1746), for example:

> O Nymph, with loosely-flowing hair,
> With buskin'd leg, and bosom bare,
> Thy waist with myrtle-girdle bound
> Thy brows with Indian feathers crown'd,
> Waving in thy snowy hand
> An all-commanding magic wand . . .
>
> [ll. 9–14]

In the case of the midcentury odes, we have typically an extensive allegorical description of the abstraction, in which the poet aims at visual impression by multiplying pictorial details either directly or suggestively. It is a type of personification meant to produce an effect of dramatic and visible presence, as if the abstraction were a sentient being. The distinctly non–Lockean implication, further, is that the abstraction exists more or less independently of the poet's mind, and that he is therefore a kind of mediator between it and his audience—he rendering it accessible in the terms of ordinary human apprehension.

Personification of the kind that Johnson illustrates offers no help to the reader who might want to turn into a spectator. But personification in Collins or Gray or Warton offers just that, and the device is enlarged far beyond its limits of role in the Dryden–Pope–Johnson tradition, such that by means of it the poet may find not merely a way of speaking from time to time, but also a subject and a theme. Johnson will allow declamation to roar in a single half-line. But for Collins, in the *Ode to Evening* (1747), the personification of the idea of evening is a way of making a poem, and a way too of seeing and knowing something as we have not quite seen or known it before:

> O Nymph reserv'd, while now the bright-hair'd sun
> Sits in yon western tent, whose cloudy skirts,
>> With brede ethereal wove,
>> O'erhang his wavy bed:
> Now air is hush'd, save where the weak-ey'd bat,
> With short shrill shriek flits by on leathern wing,
>> Or where the Beetle winds
>> His small but sullen horn,
> As oft he rises 'midst the twilight path,
> Against the pilgrim borne in heedless hum:
>> Now teach me, Maid compos'd,
>> To breathe some soften'd strain,
> Whose numbers stealing thro' thy darkning vale,
> May not unseemly with its stillness suit,
>> As musing slow, I hail
>> Thy genial lov'd return!
>
> [ll. 5–20]

Collins is describing the scene at evening, to be sure, but details like the "leathern wing" of the bat suggest that it is not the same scene everyone would describe. Yet everyone certainly knows what is meant by the abstract word "evening." This is only to say that Collins, by particularizing evening, inevitably creates his own meaning for it and is himself the most important part of the scene he describes. Collins, according to Chapin,

> would think of his personifications as, in some sort, evocations in "sensible" form of those ideas of the supreme mind which "originally gave birth to Nature." These evocations would owe their ultimate existence to the world of praeternatural reality in so far as they represented the poet's visionary insight into the realm of archetypal "ideas." Such vision could be attained only through the aid of divine inspiration. . . .[10]

By personifying abstractions, Collins may deliver up a vision of their eternal forms, making them represent something more than mere "fictions of the mind."[11] Johnson, on the other hand, sure of the radical distinction between words and things, depends on the fact that all men know what his abstractions mean before he might personify them, or regardless of his personification of them. They mean what all men agree they mean, so long at least as they remain ideas without being turned into things. Once that happens, though, they have left the public domain to become someone's private property, ceasing also to be instruments of communication.

### PERSONIFICATION IN THE CHURCHILLIAN PROGRAM: SATIRIC SELF-EXPRESSION

The two attitudes represented by Collins and Johnson are mingled distinctively in Churchill. Like Johnson, he is inclined to work hard at epigrammatic effects requiring a "metaphorical" personification to achieve the necessary compression: "Who often, but without success, have pray'd / For *apt* ALLITERATION'S artful aid . . ."[12] And like Collins, Churchill habitually apostrophizes abstractions, insinuating thereby a private and special relationship between poet and abstraction totally out of keeping with the impersonal or public terms in which Dryden, Pope, or Johnson personify abstractions—though it must be admitted that the later Pope sometimes approaches a similar effect of proprietary invocation when he speaks, say, of Truth as guarding the poet and sanctifying the line. But indeed it is from the later Pope that Churchill mainly learns:

> Is this the Land, where, in some Tyrant's reign,
> When a weak, wicked Ministerial train,
> The tools of pow'r, the slaves of int'rest, planned
> Their Country's ruin, and with bribes unman'd
> Those wretches, who, ordain'd in Freedom's cause,
> Gave up our liberties, and sold our laws;
> When Pow'r was taught by Meanness where to go.
> Nor dar'd to love the Virtue of a foe;
> When, like a lep'rous plague, from the foul head
> To the foul heart her sores Corruption spread,

Her iron arm when stern Oppression rear'd,
And Virtue, from her broad base shaken, fear'd
The scourge of Vice; when, impotent and vain,
Poor Freedom bow'd the neck to Slav'ry's chain . . .

[*The Author*, ll. 73–86]

What one notices above all in Churchill, though, is the startling adaptability and recurrence of the personification device. He evokes by means of it a curious, ghostlike world of the forms and figures of virtues, vices, influences, emotions, ideals—all variously at war or in combination with each other or projected onto his enemies or himself. Churchill, more than any other contemporary satirist, developed a program for turning the personified abstraction to the purposes of satire. That is not to say his contemporaries do not employ the device satirically. The hero of Smart's *Hilliad*, for instance, is

Conducted by a glorious cavalcade;
Pert Petulance the first attracts his eye,
And drowsy Dulness slowly saunters by,
With Malice old, and Scandal ever new,
And neutral Nonsense, neither false nor true,
Infernal Falsehood next approach'd the band
With * * * and the koran in her hand

.   .   .   .   .   .   .   .   .   .   .

Next spiteful Enmity, gangren'd at heart,
Presents a dagger and conceals a dart.
On th' earth crawls Flatt'ry with her bosom bare,
And Vanity sails over him in air.

[ll. 80–92]

Robert Lloyd's poem *The Progress of Envy* (1751),[13] which is about William Lauder's attempt to prove Milton a plagiarist, is an odd mixture of Spenser and topical satire. Written in Spenserian stanzas, it tells how Envy "left precipitate her Stygian throne" to destroy the happiness of others; leagued with Malice and Lauder, Envy devises an assault on Milton which fails miserably. What is interesting about the piece is the attempt to use Spenser's richly visualized personification for the purposes of satire. The intended victim, Lauder, is completely swallowed up in the picture of Envy's progress; or to put it another way, the pictorial qualities of the allegory obscure its meaning. But of course the meaning must eventually emerge from the scene clearly if the point of the ridicule is to get across.

Aside from rather isolated examples like these, however, none of the midcentury poets carries the technique of personification to the limits in satire that Churchill does. It is true that the technique in Churchill is overwhelmingly instrumental—that in other words, Churchill seldom personifies abstractions simply because the abstraction is inherently interesting—and if we divide the personified abstracton as Chapin does into "fictions of the mind" and "objects of sight," then Churchill's abstractions will mostly fall into the former category.

Because the dramatic potential is much greater in the abstraction as an "object of sight," however, Churchill sometimes departs from his usual practice of stripping the abstraction almost bare of modifiers and introduces a Spenserian train of more fully specified abstractions whose principal appeal is to the eye. In *The Ghost* (bk. 4, ll. 1643–1796) there is a lengthy procession of these abstract "objects of sight." For example,

> With looks, where dread command was plac'd,
> And Sov'reign Pow'r by Pride disgrac'd,
> Where, loudly witnessing a mind
> Of savage more than human kind,
> Not chusing to be lov'd, but fear'd,
> Mocking at right, MISRULE appear'd,
> With eyeballs glaring fiery red
> Enough to strike beholders dead,
> Gnashing his teeth, and in a flood
> Pouring corruption froth and blood
> From his chaf'd jaws; without remorse
> Whipping, and spurring on his horse,
> Whose sides, in their own blood embay'd,
> E'en to the bone were open laid,
> Came TYRANNY; disdaining awe,
> And trampling over *Sense* and *Law*
> One thing and only one He knew,
> One object only would pursue,

> Tho' Less (so low doth Passion bring)
> Than man, he would be more than King.
>
> [bk. 4, ll. 1759–78]

Here in this striking passage the force of the personification is almost entirely visual and dramatic. Personified Tyranny is a tyrant on horseback whose cruelty and blind ambition are exemplified in the material terms of spur and bone, Churchill having simply applied the abstract name to one of the many particular instances out of which the idea of tyranny is abstracted.

The abstraction can also be visualized as an example or victim of itself, as in Spenser's figure of Despair, personified as a man continually trying to commit suicide, or as in the *Ode to Fear* (1747), where Collins pictures Fear as a frightened man:

> Ah *Fear*! Ah frantic *Fear*!
> I see, I see Thee near.
> I know thy hurried Step, thy haggard Eye!
> Like Thee I start, like Thee disorder'd fly . . .
>
> [ll. 5–8]

Churchill too makes some use of the self-victimizing personification. *The Duellist* begins with a series of them, as

> AMBITION, who, when waking, dreams
> Of mighty, but phantastic, schemes . . .
>
> [bk. 1, ll. 7–8]

or

> JEALOUSY, his quick eye half-closed,
> With watchings worn, reluctant doz'd,
> And, mean distrust not quite forgot,
> Slumber'd as if he slumber'd not.
>
> [bk. 1, ll. 23–26]

*The Duellist* is one of the very few poems in which Churchill's personal presence is not a dominating force. This poem represents a conscious attempt on the part of the satirist to distance himself from his subject, to depend more on his powers of "invention" than on his powers of speaking. All of Book 2, for example, is an historical allegory on the already well worn theme of the decay of liberty in England. The "characters" of the action are personified abstractions who flourish, contend with each other, or suffer defeat as Churchill's story requires. The theme of that particular book is the usurpation of the temple of Liberty by "Statecraft," and as far as satire is concerned, it is a good test case for the personified abstraction. Is it possible to sustain a satiric purpose in this kind of poem?

In *The Duellist* the satirist does not overtly intrude on the scene, but on the other hand, the scene is hardly what we could call realistic. Churchill distances himself from the scene by objectifying his mental phenomena, his "fictions of the mind," turning them into seemingly autonomous actors in a drama—but only seemingly, since what appears to be a "fable" is really a dramatization of his own opinions. His ideas, personified, in effect act out his thought. As in *Gotham*, with its liberating device of the hypothetical situation (If I were King), Churchill relies on a controlling device in *The Duellist* which enables him to express himself in more or less complete intellectual freedom. This is the simple expedient of personifying his ideas—thus attributing to them some measure of literary objectivity—and then bringing them freely into the same relationships with each other that they have in his mind:

> LIBERTY fled, her Friends withdrew,
> Her Friends, a faithful, chosen few;
> HONOUR in grief threw up, and SHAME,
> Cloathing herself with HONOUR'S name,
> Usurp'd his station; on the throne,
> Which LIBERTY once call'd her own,
>
> .   .   .   .   .   .   .   .   .   .   .
>
> For ev'ry darker purpose fit,
> Behold in triumph STATE-CRAFT sit.
>
> [bk. 2, ll. 531–42]

As far as the matter of free self-expression is concerned, the personified abstraction is an ideal device for Churchill. It excludes external reality as thoroughly as it can possibly be excluded, giving us instead a shadowy dramatization of disembodied Churchillian thoughts.

Because the personified abstraction seemingly links two different worlds—that of external, substantive reality and that of internal ideas —there is always a threat that it will break apart. Ideas are one thing, after all, and people are another; to turn ideas into people, even figuratively, will call the whole relationship between subjective and objective phenomena into question.

Churchill's attitude toward abstractions is complicated. He is something of a nominalist, especially in his treatment of the traditional Augustan abstractions like nature or reason or sense. And yet he also regularly apostrophizes abstractions in a style that is not typically Augustan. In his apostrophe to Fancy in *The Ghost* (bk. 4, ll. 289–658), he expresses a specifically *personal* relationship to Fancy, stressing its influence on him in particular; in that one respect it might have been written by Collins. The same personal emphasis characterizes every other important apostrophe in Churchill's poetry. In *The Prophecy of Famine*, Churchill, playing Edmund-redivivus, adopts the divine patronage of the goddess Nature as his especially: "Thou, NATURE, are *my* goddess—to thy law / Myself I dedicate . . ." (ll. 93–94). And of Independence he says,

> Tho' Thou, Alas! art out of fashion grown,
> Tho' All despise Thee, I will not despise,
> Nor live one moment longer than I prize
> Thy presence, and enjoy; by angry Fate
> Bow'd down, and almost crush'd, *Thou* cam'st, tho' late,
> *Thou* cam'st upon me, like a second birth,
> And made me know what life was truly worth.
> [*Independence*, ll. 510–16]

Although the form of Churchill's apostrophe suggests perhaps that he is addressing something beyond or above himself, the fact that an ideal like Nature or Independence is associated so exclusively and privately with himself argues what I have already suggested—that Churchill's values are finally represented as having a meaning which is mainly subjective and personal.

For Churchill, consequently, most (and probably all) abstractions have no real existence outside his mind. They are names. Sometimes

he will drop an intriguing hint to that effect, as when he personifies
Candour in the *Epistle to William Hogarth* only in order to quarrel
with her. Or this on Reason, from *The Ghost*:

> Within the brain's most secret cells,
> A certain *Lord Chief Justice* dwells
> Of sov'reign pow'r, whom One and All,
> With common Voice, we REASON call;
> Tho', for the purposes of Satire,
> A name in Truth is no great Matter . . .
>
> [bk. 4, ll. 125–30]

Similarly, Honor is

> a Word, which all the *Nine*
> Would be much puzzled to define—
> HONOUR—a Word which torture mocks
> And might confound a thousand LOCKES . . .
>
> [bk. 4, ll. 897–900]

This nominalistic trend in Churchill's thinking can partly be explained by his insistence on a theory of moral decay. The old virtues
are gone, things are not what they used to be. As a matter of fact,
Churchill devotes an entire poem (*The Times*) to the *O tempora*
theme. His readiness to personify abstractions serves him well in developing this idea, because very often a "true" or "original" virtue
will be contrasted with its latter-day descendant. Once upon a time
Truth was an absolute thing, but now it is debauched and relative:
Eternal Truth has become "a downright *City* Truth" (*The Ghost*, bk.
2, l. 198). The same sort of thing happens to poor Liberty when Statecraft violates her temple in Book 2 of *The Duellist*.

Churchill, like certain of his contemporaries, is in a quandary. He
is not sure that he can know anything beyond his own feelings, and as
a result, sensibility and understanding, Fancy and Reason, are treated
ambiguously. Churchill is prepared to think, for example, that men
actually do become what they believe they are if only because there is
no way to contradict their belief. These are fresh ideas, and they give
the satirist special difficulties because he has to deal with them using
traditional forms.

*The Ghost* is a good illustration of Churchill's epistemology (if the term is not overdignified). In this poem he ridicules the affair of the Cock Lane Ghost by reducing it to nothing, or to a production merely of the collective popular fancy. Churchill solemnly records the folly brought on by superstition, credulity, and curiosity, "whose rage," he writes, "Must be indulg'd at the expence / Of *Judgment, Truth,* and *Common Sense* . . ." (bk. 1, ll. 473–74). How can we believe, he asks, that nature would suspend "her usual course" and vary "from the stated plan" (bk. 1, ll. 446–47) in order to produce one freak of nature like a rabbit-breeding Mary Tofts? The answer lies in the ease with which almost anything can break the tenuous hold of the senses on the understanding. Sensible evidence is never much of a match for the wonderful falsehoods that Fancy is capable of creating. Churchill's long essay on this subject in *The Ghost* (bk. 4, ll. 289–658), is earnestly ambiguous and uncertain. In it he enlarges sincerely on the theme of the power of Fancy, but he also satirizes the victims of Fancy. Indeed, they are only victims in the eyes of others who see them as they are. As far as the victim himself is concerned, he "Mocks boasted vain *Reality,* / And *Is,* whate'er he wants to Be." (bk. 4, ll. 309–10). So long as Churchill locates reality in the individual consciousness, it really doesn't matter, then, if the world takes a self-deluded man for a fool.

In this passage on Fancy is one of Churchill's most vicious portraits, directed at just such a man, the "Whiffle" who

> riots, tho' he loves not waste,
> Whores without lust, drinks without taste.
> Acts without sense, talks without thought,
> Does every thing but what he ought . . .
> [bk. 4, ll. 538–41]

That, at any rate, is how Churchill the satirist sees him. Whiffle, however, sees himself as "more than human" (l. 565), and the mystery of it all is that the deception is somehow more "real" than the truth. So it becomes possible for Churchill to ridicule other victims of Fancy and include himself among them. Each of us is confined to his own point of view, now an observer, now the observed. Your point of view is no better than mine, even if I am Whiffle and you are the rest of the world:

> By his own Sense and Feelings taught,
> In speech as lib'ral as in thought,
> Let ev'ry Man enjoy his whim;
> What's He to Me, or I to him?

[bk. 4, ll. 213–16]

Churchill never doubts that the abstractions he personifies are anything but "fictions of the mind," and to that extent he is in line with Locke and Johnson. Unlike Locke and Johnson, though, he treats them as fictions of his own mind. It is a case of a slight shift in emphasis bringing about a great shift in thinking. Language for Churchill is a vehicle of personal expression, not communication. "What's He to Me, or I to him?" Locke's theory and Johnson's practice tell us that if the proper purpose of words is communication, the most proper words must be general words. But generalization, conceivably at least, can be put to work in the context of an expressive theory of language. This is how Churchill converts a traditional technique into the instrument of an untraditional satiric program, which is to say he generalizes himself. We do not sense the weight of "representative human experience" behind Churchill's generalizations, as F. R. Leavis did in the case of Johnson.[14] "Personifications and generalizations," says Donald Davie, "are justifiable according as they are 'worked for.' "[15] Churchill does not work for his personifications because he is willing to have one particular incident—say the duel between John Wilkes and Samuel Martin which occasioned the writing of *The Duellist*—stand for the triumph of Statecraft over Liberty. Even so, personification in Churchill is a powerful tool of satire, if only because it forces us to go outside the work itself in order to have any perspective on the judgments made within it.

### PERSONIFICATION IN SATIRE AFTER CHURCHILL

If Locke may be said to have led us this far in understanding the role of personification in eighteenth-century satire, Hume takes us the rest of the way. In 1757 he wrote:

It is indeed obvious that writers of all nations and all ages concur in applauding justice, humanity, magnanimity, prudence, veracity; and in blaming the opposite qualities. Even poets and other authors whose compositions are chiefly calculated to please the imagination are yet found, from Homer down to Fénelon, to inculcate the same moral precepts, and to bestow their applause and blame on the same virtues and vices. This great unanimity is usually ascribed to the influence of plain reason, which in all these cases maintains similar sentiments in all men and prevents those controversies to which the abstract sciences are so much exposed. So far as the unanimity is real, this account may be admitted as satisfactory. But we must also allow that some part of the seeming harmony in morals may be accounted for from the very nature of language. The word *Virtue*, with its equivalent in every tongue, implies praise; as that of *vice* does blame. And no one, without the most obvious and grossest impropriety, could affix reproach to a term which in general acceptation is understood in a good sense, or bestow applause where the idiom requires disapprobation. . . .

The merit of delivering true general precepts in ethics is indeed very small. Whoever recommends any moral virtues really does no more than is implied in the terms themselves.[16]

Hume makes this observation in connection with the subject of taste, but its wider implications are clear enough: that the true basis of the associations evoked by moral abstractions, such as Virtue, Vice, Reason, and Nature, lies not in morals but in language. This illustrates a certain doubt as to what is really meant by such abstractions: do they in fact mean what they have always been thought to mean?

As far as the actual poetic practice of the later century is concerned, the habit of personifying abstractions weakens dramatically—although one must concede that it could scarcely be expected not to have weakened some following its extraordinary hold on poetic usage at midcentury. But more than merely weakening, it virtually disappears. Not much can be made of negative evidence, admittedly, but it seems safe to say that this development most likely reflects an attitude of doubt of the sort we see in Hume; and hence a reluctance to stylize the abstraction in such a way as to emphasize the very thing in respect of which it is doubted—its basis in something other than words.

Of the two traditions that can be seen as leading up to and, to some extent, joining in Churchill's use of personifications, one, that of the strictly rhetorical personification, simply plays out, while the other type of personification leads toward increasingly concrete exemplification, such that it loses its force as an abstraction.

As for the first, one notices in Chatterton's satire a use of personified abstractions that is much less extensive than Churchill's but essentially similar: he does not particularly "work for" a general force in his abstractions but rather calls upon them in obviously partisan contexts, as in *Kew Gardens*, where one of the government hireling poets "borrows Persecution's Scourge of Bute."[17] Or this sort of thing, from the *Consuliad*, a poem depicting, in mock–Miltonic style, a common brawl among a group of contemporary politicians assembled at a dinner: "And now confusion spread her ghastly plume: / And faction separates the noisy room."[18] There are moments—usually only that—when the device is employed with a skill and effect that takes us back to Johnson, as in Cowper's lines,

> Where obstinacy takes his sturdy stand,
> To disconcert what policy has plann'd;
> Where policy is busied all night long
> In setting right what faction has set wrong;
> Where flails of oratory thresh the floor,
> That yields them chaff and dust, and nothing more.[19]

But in satire of the later years of our period, generally speaking, the personified abstraction is seldom introduced and used unreflectingly. That is, certain abstractions retain their personified force (especially "Satire"—obviously enough—and "Liberty"), but the writer adopts a special point of view toward them. Usually, like Churchill, he regards them as "lost" to the modern world. This practice is of course after the manner of Pope in his later satires: "*Religion* blushing veils her sacred fires, / And unawares *Morality* expires."[20] Paul Whitehead had also written often in this vein:

> Sick of a land where *Virtue* dwells no more,
> See LIBERTY prepar'd to quit our shore!
> Pruning her pinions, on yon beacon'd height

The Goddess stands, and meditates her flight;
Now spreads her wings, unwilling yet to fly,
Again o'er BRITAIN casts a pitying eye . . .[21]

It becomes a clearly dominant theme later on, when we find Peter
Pindar writing a poem called *Liberty's Last Squeak*, and Byron asking
it of England,

Would she be proud, or boast herself the free,
Who is but first of slaves? The nations are
In prison,—but the gaoler, what is he?
No less a victim to the bolt and bar.
Is the poor privilege to turn the key
Upon the captive, Freedom? [22]

The theme had become so familiar later in the century, in fact, that
one anonymous writer pretends to be out of patience with it:

When learning, honesty, and merit,
Love of our country, public spirit,
Virtue, sobriety, frugality,
Religion, chastity, morality,
The precious value of our time,
And divers other words that rhyme,
Are banish'd from the earth—what then?
Will writing bring 'em back again?

This is from an anti-sentimentalist poem entitled *The Optimist; or,
Satire in Good-Humour*.[23] Poetically it is a rather horrible piece, but
it does illustrate how sometimes the personified abstraction comes in
for burlesque treatment. Having made the point that the abstractions
he names are banished from the earth—implying that these are really
only "words that rhyme"—the author writes,

Haply these gentry once appear'd,
Ere master Jovey had a beard,
When Juno was a little virgin,
Nor felt that certain something urging . . .
In short, ere churches had a steeple,
Or this same world was fill'd with people . . .

They never existed, in other words. Or if they did, then

> So great has been th'increase of sinning,
> That the whole cargo long ago,
> Shipp'd off, and are forgotten now.

Peter Pindar also likes to take an insouciant approach to the abstractions he occasionally personifies:

> Oft have I dipp'd in golden praise the pen,
> Writing *such handsome things* about Great Men,
> That Candour's eye-balls have been seen to wonder.[24]

The effect in something like this is to make us think of Candour only as a conventional literary allusion. Certainly we are not made to feel the personification itself has any very serious basis outside literature.

Besides such comic "diminishing" of the personified abstraction, there is also a tendency during the period to personify certain abstractions in order to ridicule their meaninglessness. Churchill does this, and so also does Chatterton when he writes sarcastically about revealed religion:

> Religion's but Opinion's bastard Son
> A perfect Mystry, more than three in One
> Tis Fancy all, Distempers of the Mind . . .[25]

But here as in Churchill the question must arise as to the propriety of calling one abstraction an empty name without calling all abstractions empty names.

In this connection Canning and Frere's *New Morality* is an engrossing example. For here there is no taking the meaning of an abstraction for granted but rather—quite the opposite—a felt need to separate the different meanings that the name of an abstraction may acquire, to distinguish between the reality and the name merely of a moral virtue:

> If Vice appall thee,—if thou view with awe
> Insults that brave, and crimes that 'scape the law;—
> Yet may the specious bastard brood, which claim
> A spurious homage under Virtue's name,
> Sprung from that parent of ten thousand crimes,
> The *New Philosophy* of modern times,

Yet, these may rouse thee!—with unsparing hand,
Oh, lash the vile impostures from the land!

—First, stern Philosophy:—not she who dries
The orphan's tears, and wipes the widow's eyes;
Not she, who, sainted Charity her guide,
Of British bounty pours the annual tide:—
But *French* Philanthropy;—whose boundless mind
Glows with the general love of all mankind;
Philanthropy,—beneath whose baneful sway
Each patriot passion sinks and dies away.[26]

Likewise Justice:

Not she in British Courts that takes her stand,
The dawdling balance dangling in her hand,
Adjusting punishments to fraud and vice,
With scrupulous quirks, and disquisition nice:—
But firm, erect, with keen reverted glance,
The avenging angel of regenerate France,
Who visits ancient sins on modern times,
And punishes the Pope for Caesar's crimes.

[ll. 160–67]

These lines, despite their confident tone, might almost be considered a satirical exercise on Hume's theme of the confused interplay between morality itself and the language of morality. In any case, the assumption upon which the lines are written is one that sooner or later must be incompatible with the practice of personifying abstractions. It probably is significant that this poem constitutes the last important instance of personification in satire, and that in this instance the personifications are themselves the objects of the satire, which is seeking to explode their claim to a valid meaning. Canning's verses on Sensibility are too good not to repeat in full:

Next comes a gentler Virtue.—Ah! beware
Lest the harsh verse her shrinking softness scare.
Visit her not too roughly;—the warm sigh
Breathes on her lips;—the tear-drop gems her eye.
Sweet Sensibility, who dwells enshrined
In the fine foldings of the feeling mind;—

With delicate Mimosa's sense endued,
Who shrinks instinctive from a hand too rude;
Or, like the *anagallis*, prescient flower,
Shuts her soft petals at the approaching shower.

Sweet child of sickly Fancy!—her of yore
From her loved France Rousseau to exile bore;
And, while midst lakes and mountains wild he ran,
Full of himself, and shunn'd the haunts of man,
Taught her o'er each lone vale and Alpine steep
To lisp the story of his wrongs, and weep;
Taught her to cherish still in either eye,
Of tender tears a plentiful supply,
And pour them in the brooks that babbled by;—
—Taught by nice scales to mete her feelings strong,
False by degrees, and exquisitely wrong;—
—For the crushed beetle *first*,—the widow'd dove,
And all the warbled sorrows of the grove;—
*Next* for poor suff'ring *guilt*;—and *last* of all,
For Parents, Friends, a King and Country's fall.

[ll. 115–39]

Here I would stress the extent to which Sensibility, in being made the "object" of the satire, is necessarily "objectified" or presented visually and dramatically. This is the other main direction in which the personification moves in later satire; the direction, that is, in which the abstraction more or less becomes a specific example of itself.

The figures of Fun, Superstition, and Hypocrisy in Burns's *Holy Fair* belong in this category, as does (even more clearly) his allusion to "Frailty" in the *Address to the Unco Guid*:

Ye high, exalted, virtuous Dames,
    Ty'd up in godly laces,
Before ye gie poor *Frailty* names,
    Suppose a change o' cases;
A dear-lov'd lad, convenience snug,
    A treacherous inclination—
But let me whisper i' your lug,
    Ye're aiblins nae temptation.

[ll. 41–48]

The whole idea here, indeed, is that "Frailty" cannot be understood except as it is exemplified in the individual case: "A dear-lov'd lad, convenience sung." But this is of course to leave the abstraction relatively without a status of meaning.

There is a similar type of pressure on the abstraction to resolve itself into a concrete example in Byron's personification of jealousy in *Beppo* —for he is not speaking of Jealousy, period, but of a particular jealousy:

> Their jealousy (if they are ever jealous)
>     Is of a fair complexion altogether,
> Not like that sooty devil of Othello's
>     Which smothers women in a bed of feather,
> But worthier of these much more jolly fellows,
>     When weary of the matrimonial tether;
> His head for such a wife no mortal bothers,
> But takes at once another, or another's.
>
> [st. 18]

This tendency harmonizes with the overall context of Byron's comic-realistic manner, in which abstract ideas generally are the subject of skeptical inquiry, the burden of which is to set their presumptive meaning hopelessly at odds with the concrete cases they are supposed to subsume (the idea of "Glory" in the Siege of Ismail cantos in *Don Juan*, for example).

Byron, unlike Churchill, is largely free of the necessity to represent abstractions seriously. And whereas Churchill very often expresses himself through the abstraction, Byron likes to express himself deliberately in spite of it. We should perhaps want to ask ourselves why there is so much personification in Churchill, as against so little use of it in satire afterwards. Any answer to that question would also, I think, answer the more general question of why the sudden burst of personification in midcentury poetry as a whole. My own view is that this phenomenon represents an attempt to engage an older device of style in a program of poetical self-expression for which it is not well suited; hence the seemingly very exaggerated or distorted use of it (though any complete study of the subject—and it is a most interesting one—should, taking it on its own terms, produce a more positive emphasis).

In any event, the practice appears to run a losing race with the increasingly critical attitude toward abstractions and what they "really" mean, for the writers evidently discover that things are somehow more "real" than ideas. The exemplification of meaning in concrete rather than abstract terms is, so to speak, the other side of the coin, and is the subject of the following chapter.

# CHAPTER 4

# Satiric Illustration and the "Scene" of Satire

I HAVE MADE up the not very exacting term "satiric illustration" as a way of gathering together various of the characteristic methods by which the satirist may exemplify or "illustrate" his meaning, as in description, analogies, and narration. The proper opposite of the term would be "satiric statement," referring simply to the direct declaration of meaning: "Stiff in Opinions, always in the wrong." There is a certain risk in making this distinction, in that it implies perhaps too strongly that satire can be considered as consisting of illustration and of that which is illustrated; obviously that is not so, and in fact is hardly ever so, but the distinction does provide a useful pair of categories under which a great many satires can legitimately be compared.

More particularly, then, this chapter gives an account of the way in which this "illustrative" or "representational" aspect of satire is understood and adapted during the period. And in further qualification I would add that I am focusing not so much on the illustrative material itself, i.e., the types of things described or fictionalized, as on its function and role in the satire. In this connection there are two especially important considerations, one having to do with the nature of the relationship between declarative and illustrative expressions of meaning, the other with the degree to which a description or fiction serves the purpose of satire, as against its serving some other purpose.

Sometimes description and narrative can be employed with enough consistency of purpose to create a definite "scene" in satire. Such is obviously the case in a work like *Gulliver's Travels,* as also in works like the great Augustan mock-epics, where whole symbolic "worlds" are projected. On the other hand, it is probably best not to try to impose the idea of a "scene" on all satires, since many of them, especially those in verse, do not really have any "scene" except in some sense that is too abstract to be very helpful. So the concept of a satiric scene, while in certain instances being the only adequate way of defining the illustrative aspect of a satire, should on the whole be carefully applied.

For another thing, literary satire, while it is certainly capable of producing dramatic visual or "scenic" effects, nevertheless does not produce them as immediately or in the same way as paintings or films; but we are in the habit of comparing the "scene" of written satire to these other forms, and sometimes we may mistakenly endow the one with the special capacities of the other. Reading about an ugly urban street scene is surely different from seeing such a scene in a painting or a film. This difference is a most intriguing subject in itself, although for these purposes it is enough to say that the distinction ought to be in our minds, and that it is confusing to talk about the "scene" of literary satire as though it were actually communicated by means of optical images instead of verbal ones.

The Augustans thought of description and metaphor in poetry as mainly existing for something other than their own sakes, as serving some purpose—decorative, illustrative, or satirically reductive. Pope, for example, speaks of true wit as figurative and ornamental only secondarily, its primary characteristic being that it describes "the naked nature" and thus "gives us back the image of our mind."[1] So also with satiric poetry, for although the satirists of the Restoration and early eighteenth century do frequently draw upon the resources of description, metaphor, animal and heroic imagery, beast fables, and other such conventions whose appeal is mainly representational rather than discursive or dialectical, they clearly do not see their satire as mainly representational in nature. For them it is more appropriately defined in terms of intention and effect; hence the reason that so many of the words they use in talking about satire have to do either with what the satirist (supposedly) has in his mind or what effect the satire (supposedly) has on the victim: indignation, virtue, honesty, fear, punishment, reform. The illustrative and representational qualities of satire, then, have particular significance only insofar as they contribute to the main business of the genre, which is satire.

The type of imagery most completely subordinated to the satiric purpose is name-calling, in which the names or images are designed to make the victim "look" bad (though not usually in a strictly visual sense). To take a simple case, if a satirist says, "Sir Roland is an ass," we have an example of a satiric metaphor—if that isn't inflating the example too much—whose vehicle, the image of the ass, has virtually no effect other than that of abuse. And in this particular case, it would really be more accurate to speak of the word "ass" as constituting an idea rather than an image, since the word in fact does not make us "see" an animal but instead puts us in mind of the idea of debasement that the word always carries when it is used in that way.

This case naturally represents an extreme, and much depends on how conventionally abusive or degrading the chosen name is, that is, the extent to which a name such as "ass" or "swine" has in certain contexts lost its capacity to register anything visual in the mind of the reader in favor of registering simply as an evaluative term. There is a third-rate anti-Puritan satire of 1655, for instance, in which the poet ridicules a preacher as a chattering magpie.[2] Most of the relatively few satiric similes and metaphors in Commonwealth ballad satires also drift toward this extreme:

> Our Churches now are purged cleane,
> From Prelats, Chapters, and the Deane,
> Who long have liv'd like Hogs.[3]

The point is not that this last line has no visual effect, because to the audience for which it was written it might well have had; but simply that the effect is completely subordinated to the main idea of the lines: that of the useless and unworthy ecclesiastics having been properly turned out.

In late seventeenth- and early eighteenth-century satire, most of the reductive or ridiculing comparisons fall into this pattern of a controlled, subordinate relationship between the vehicle, whose content is often heavily conventionalized, and the theme it is illustrating. Thus Dryden in *The Medal*, envisioning how even if the royal succession

were broken and "the *Presbyter*, puft up with spiritual Pride," should
come to power, his fellow-sectarians would eventually want the King
back anyway:

> But short shall be his Reign: his rigid Yoke
> And Tyrant Pow'r will puny Sects provoke;
> And Frogs and Toads, and all the Tadpole Train
> Will croak to Heav'n for help, from this devouring Crane.
>
> [ll. 302–5]

And Pope's

> Rufa, whose eye quick-glancing o'er the Park,
> Attracts each light gay meteor of a Spark
> Agrees as ill with Rufa studying Locke,
> As Sappho's diamonds with her dirty smock,
> Or Sappho at her toilet's greasy task,
> With Sappho fragrant at an ev'ning Mask:
> So morning Insects that in muck begun,
> Shine, buzz, and fly-blow in the setting-sun.
>
> [*Epistle to a Lady*, ll. 21–28]

On the other hand, simple, direct comparisons like these constitute
only one type of satiric illustration during the period, and that a relatively infrequent type. To return to the example of *The Medal* again,
I would point out that the kind of comparison cited above occurs three
or four times in that poem, as opposed to a much greater number of
occasions on which a comparison is made, or only implied, without a
clear mechanical separation between the two terms of the comparison:

> But this new *Jehu* spurs the hot mouth'd horse;
> Instructs the Beast to know his native force;
> To take the Bit between his teeth and fly
> To the next headlong Steep of Anarchy.
>
> [ll. 119–22]

Here the effect is allegorical in the easy mixing of abstract and concrete
fields of reference; one hesitates to call it either an abstract meaning
rendered concretely, or a concrete visualization of an abstract meaning,
because the mixing of the two is brought about as though there were
not really much difference between "abstract" and "concrete." In the

case of tropes where this difference is more definitely felt, there is usually something that advertises the "turning" of one into the other: the "like" or "as" of a simile, the remoteness of the analogy, the strength with which attention is called to one term or the other (as when the abstract idea is a very complicated one, or when the illustrative material is very specifically visualized). Here, however, the references to abstract meaning and to physical reality both take place at what W. K. Wimsatt, Jr. calls the "substantive level" of discourse, that level at which a spade is called a spade and not something more specific or more general.[4] The idea of anarchy is introduced but not qualified; it is simply "Anarchy." Nor is the description of the galloping horse and rider particularly vivid or detailed, but characteristically Augustan in Dryden's way of giving little more than their proper names to the various elements of the picture, and certainly Augustan in the diction of "Instructs the Beast to know his native force."

I have lingered over these lines from *The Medal* because this type of description, the "seeing" of things in language that speaks to us partly in abstract terms, partly in concrete, is so characteristic a feature of Augustan satire (and, for that matter, of Augustan poetry generally). Technically it would have to be called a form of figurative discourse, but the thing that particularly distinguishes it is the thoroughness of the blend between discourse and figure. There is another example at the beginning of Rochester's *Satyr against Mankind*:

> Reason, an *ignis fatuus* in the mind,
> Which, leaving light of nature, sense, behind,
> Pathless and dangerous wandering ways it takes
> Through error's fenny bogs and thorny brakes;
> Whilst the misguided follower climbs with pain
> Mountains of whimseys, heaped in his own brain;
> Stumbling from thought to thought, falls headlong down
> Into doubt's boundless sea, where, like to drown,
> Books bear him up awhile, and make him try
> To swim with bladders of philosophy . . .[5]

While strictly speaking, reason is being compared metaphorically to a will-o'the-wisp, the conventionality of the figurative resemblances

—error as a wilderness, doubt as an ocean—has the effect of making us much less aware that there *is* a figure involved. The figurative elements, indeed, are presented with the matter-of-factness of declarative statement, which perhaps accounts for the feeling one has here that description (of something concrete) and statement (of abstract ideas) are nearly the same thing. We respond to the realized "scene" in a way that is neither fully visual nor fully intellectual: does the phrase "Stumbling from thought to thought" chiefly rouse the imagination visually or conceptually?

We have the same effect, more fleetingly, in *Absalom and Achitophel* where Dryden is describing how the public "swallowed" the idea of the Popish Plot: "Not weighed or winnowed by the multitude; But swallowed in the mass, unchewed and crude" (ll. 112–13).

And for Pope, who makes more and better use of the device than any other poet of the period, this habit of "seeing" a moral meaning and then simply describing what he "sees" is second nature:

> Still round and round the Ghosts of Beauty glide,
> And haunt the places where their Honour dy'd.
> [*Epistle to a Lady*, ll. 241–42]

> Who shames a Scribler? break one cobweb thro',
> He spins the slight, self-pleasing thread anew;
> Destroy his Fib, or Sophistry; in vain,
> The Creature's at his dirty work again;
> Thron'd in the Centre of his thin designs;
> Proud of a vast Extent of flimzy lines.
> [*Epistle to Arbuthnot*, ll. 89–94]

Mock-epic imagery constitutes a third type of description associated with Augustan satire, and it is in this familiar category that we find the most spectacular range of visual effects. Here also the usual subordination of illustrative material to satiric purpose is often less apparent or direct, although generally speaking such material is still basically an instrument of the satire.

In the preface to his translation of the *Aeneid* (1697), Dryden speaks of epic similes strictly in terms of their function and affective qualities:

Similitudes, as I have said, are not for Tragedy, which is all violent, and where the Passions are in a perpetual ferment; for there they deaden where they should animate; they are not of the nature of Dialogue, unless in Comedy: A Metaphor is almost all the Stage can suffer, which is a kind of Similitude comprehended in a word. But this Figure has a contrary effect in Heroick Poetry: There 'tis employ'd to raise the Admiration, which is its proper business. And Admiration is not of so violent a nature as Fear or Hope, Compassion or Horrour, or any Concernment we can have for such or such a Person on the Stage. Not but I confess, that Similitudes and Descriptions, when drawn into an unreasonable length, must needs nauseate the Reader. Once I remember, and but once; *Virgil* makes a similitude of fourteen lines . . . But Faults are no Precedents. This I have observ'd of his Similitudes in general, that they are not plac'd, as our unobserving Criticks tell us, in the heat of any Action: But commonly in its declining: When he has warm'd us in his Description, as much as possibly he can; then, lest that warmth should languish, he renews it by some apt Similitude, which illustrates his Subject, and yet palls not his Audience.[6]

The points he makes, that the epic simile is designed to raise the admiration of the audience and function illustratively, will apply equally in reverse to mock-epic descriptions and similes, which work to excite negative feelings such as ridicule or revulsion in the audience:

> At his right hand our young *Ascanius* sate
> Rome's other hope, and pillar of the State.
> His Brows thick fogs, instead of glories, grace,
> And lambent dullness plaid around his face.
>
> [*Mac Flecknoe*, ll. 108–11]

> Sudden, a burst of thunder shook the flood.
> Lo Smedley rose, in majesty of mud!
> Shaking the horrors of his ample brows,
> And each ferocious feature grim with ooze.
>
> [*The Dunciad Variorum*, bk. 2, ll. 301–4]

Mock-epic descriptions such as these function satirically as devices of ridicule, and in that respect they are like ordinary satiric description; but they are also supposed to echo or "mock" the epic itself, trading on the purely literary expectations of the reader, which means that the author has in mind not only their effectiveness as satire but also their cleverness as allusions.

Thus the term "satiric illustration" has to be qualified in applying it to the mock-epic, where the special requirements of the genre almost always mediate between the illustrative material and whatever general satiric purpose is at work. *Mac Flecknoe* is a satire on the true-blue Protestant poet Thomas Shadwell, but the satirist must realize that purpose indirectly, by writing about Shadwell in terms that are dictated not by satire but by classical epic poetry. All this is no more than to say that the mock-epic is a form that is not wholly or always conceived of as satire; and while *Mac Flecknoe*, Garth's *Dispensary*, and the *Dunciad* are satirical, in varying degree, *The Rape of the Lock* and Gay's *The Fan* (1714) are less clearly so, and Paul Whitehead's *Gymnasiad* (1744) and Richard Owen Cambridge's *Scribleriad* (1751), in their self-conscious striving for mock-heroic purity, even less clearly so.

The effect of such diffusion of purpose is to give the satirist a freer hand in making use of illustrative material, much of which is not itself morally or satirically conceived but rather exists to establish the elaborate scene of the mock-epic. Hence the descriptions themselves frequently cannot be referred to any definite satiric purpose but must be understood as imaginative in nature; hence also, I think, the feeling since Joseph Warton's time that a poem like the *Rape of the Lock* is somehow more "poetic" than, say, the *Epistle to Bathurst*. There is an insistence on the visual aspect of the "scene" that is ordinarily not associated with satire. Such lines in the *Rape of the Lock* as "But now secure the painted Vessel glides, / The Sun-beams trembling on the floating Tydes . . ." (canto 2, ll. 47–48), and "Here living Teapots stand, one Arm held out, / One bent; the Handle this, and that the Spout . . ." (canto 4, ll. 49–50) work mainly to add to our sense of the exaggerated and fantastic scenery of the poem. These images may combine to create a "world" that has in its overall aspect an ironically or symbolically satiric meaning. But they do not primarily serve to communicate or "describe" a meaning, like the "Who shames a Scribbler" lines quoted above. Other examples would include the description of the raising of the altar to Disease in the *Dispensary* (bk. 3, ll. 83–94), the grove of Venus and her workshop-cave in Gay's *The Fan* (bk. 1, ll. 93–142), or the scene at the games in the *Dunciad* where Curll tries to snatch the prize, the effigy of Moore-Smythe, which then, in a delightful piece of description, vanishes (bk. 2, ll. 109–20).

With the mock-epic we come also to the matter of narrative and fictional elements. The "story" aspect of Augustan satire is obviously a big subject, and again, as in the case of satiric description, I want to consider it only in terms of function and effect rather than actual content.[7] In Augustan satire, that is, storytelling, like description, is usually illustrative, and the purely representational value of action, character, and dialogue is subordinate, in various degrees, to the part these elements play in communicating satiric meaning.

The use of anecdote in formal satire comes to mind as perhaps the most clear-cut example of this. Edward Young is particularly in the habit of embellishing his themes with stories which by their brevity and generality hardly break the movement of stated meaning, as in this one ridiculing the illiterate bibliophile:

> On buying books Lorenzo long was bent,
> But found at length that it reduc'd his rent;
> His farms were flown; when, lo! a sale comes on,
> A choice collection! what is to be done?
> He sells his last; for he the whole will buy;
> Sells ev'n his house; nay wants whereon to lie:
> So high the gen'rous ardour of the man
> For Romans, Greeks, and Orientals ran.
> When terms were drawn, and brought him by the clerk,
> Lorenzo sign'd the bargain—with his mark.
> Unlearned men of books assume the care,
> As eunuchs are the guardians of the fair.[8]

There are also the illustrative anecdotes in Pope's *Moral Essays*, ranging from the six-line story of Euclio's miserly death in the *Epistle to Cobham* (ll. 256–61) to the lengthy tale of Sir Balaam (*Epistle to Bathurst*, ll. 339–402), which with its particularization of character and incident has a quality of short-story fiction and seems to look forward to George Crabbe.

A distinction can be made between the satire that contains a story or anecdote, as in the examples just cited, and the satire that is itself a story. If we set aside the mock-heroic satire as a special case, relatively few poems in the years between the Restoration and the death of Pope qualify both as satire and as tales or fables. In those that do qualify as both, the story is "controlled" in some important respect by the satiric intention: by means of allegory, which draws our attention away from the story to the satiric meaning, or by using convention-alized stories with very well established patterns of meaning and response, or by distorting or contriving the reality that the story "represents" so as to maximize satiric effect. It may be simply that the two existed in such well-defined terms as distinct genres, quite independent of each other, that someone starting to write a poem would be likely to conceive of his intentions in terms of one or the other but not the two together. The fable usually requires a level of generality that is inconsistent with satire. Gay, for instance, talks about "lashing vice" in his fables, but also says that he does it "in general fiction": that is, in stories where a proverbial perspective is given to the follies and vices of men by having animals act them out.[9] Obviously this formula will not apply to every case. Sometimes the fable does become satire, as in Thomas Yalden's *Aesop at Court* (1702), which has a political application. Occasionally too there is the fable that translates allegorically into satire, such as William King's *The Eagle and the Robin* (1709), an "apologue," as he calls it, about the change in Queen Anne's ministry. And of course Swift must be considered as writing satire in his fables, where the story quite clearly exists for the sake of the satire; in the *Progress of Poetry*, in fact, which compares a goose and a Grub-street poet, it is hard to know whether to call the poem a fable with a satiric application or an elaborate satiric simile.

Sometimes the Augustan satirist will represent a character as actually speaking, although the effect is seldom what we think of as dramatic or fictional characterization. There are soliloquies, indirect quotations, overheard phrases, dialogues, and conversations, the representation of which is either very highly selective or completely fanciful and outside the mimetic rules of probability. We get speech, then, that does not really present or reveal "character" as in plays or novels but which instead exemplifies and advances the satiric case that is being built.

This is peculiarly characteristic of seventeenth-century political satires, where the trick is to have the person or type-character who is being satirized say impossibly self-incriminating things about himself. Often an entire ballad will consist of such a "speech," as in *Tyburne Cheated* (1661), a first-person plural apostrophe to the scaffold by three regicides who had been sentenced to be dragged there from their prison each year on the anniversary of Charles' execution. The balladeer thinks they should have been executed themselves, but he makes them say so:

> Did we not doe a pretty thing,
> To *Murder* a Religious *King*:
> Oh! how we quafft his guiltless blood,
> He onely dy'd for being *good*;
> Whilst all the Punishment we had
> Was but to live, for being *bad*;
> If this be all we must incurr,
> Who would not be a *Murtherer* . . .[10]

John Oldham's *Satires upon the Jesuits* make elaborate use of the convention. Only one of the four satires, the second, represents the satirist himself as speaking. In the first, the ghost of Henry Garnet appears to a secret meeting of Jesuits after the murder of Sir Edmund Berry Godfrey and in his address to them—beginning "By hell 'twas bravely done!"—lays bare the horrifying "truth" about the Popish Plot. Satire 3 is a dramatization of Loyola's dying speech to his soldier–clerics, exhorting them in the most lurid, self-condemning terms to press on with their unholy mission, to "stick at no crime." Satire 4 brings a wooden statue of Loyola to life, and we hear him reveal the truth—not his version, of course, but the satirist's—about the venality and mumbo-jumbo inside his church.

The effect reminds one of Chaucer's Pardoner, whose character is either not really dramatized at all, except nominally, so that what we are actually hearing is Chaucer talking about the Pardoner as though it were the Pardoner himself speaking, or else he is inhumanly candid about himself. It is a question of degree, of course, since the most acceptably "realistic" dramatization of a character is also a selective, stylized representation that can eventually be traced back to the author's intentions about how he wished that character to appear. The difference is simply that in satiric representations of the kind I have been considering, the illusionist conventions (like the rule of probability or consistency) are much slighter, almost nonexistent.

A somewhat more "realistic" representation of speech is usual in satires that treat manners and social life. Here the satirist makes his point by being carefully selective, as Young in indirect quotation of the "languid lady": "Fan! hood! glove! scarf! is her laconic style!"[11] Likewise Pope's Sir Plume in *The Rape of the Lock*:

> 'My Lord, why, what the Devil?
> Z——ds! damn the Lock! 'fore Gad, you must be civil!
> Plague on't! 'tis past a Jest—nay prithee, Pox!
> Give her the Hair!'—he spoke, and rapp'd his Box.
> [canto 4, ll. 127–30]

In considering the matter of satire which is itself a story, I passed over the mock-epic as a special case but should like now to return to it. Obviously this is the most important type of verse satire in narrative form during the period; its plot, like its imagery, serves the purposes partly of satire, partly of epic allusion, and is not "realistic" in the way the plot of the domestic verse tale or the novel is.

The narrative line of a mock-epic is (by definition) thoroughly conventionalized: an old "action" familiarized by literary experience rather than a contemporary plot about which the reader has fewer expectations. In its conventionality the plot of the mock-epic calls relatively little attention to itself except as it is applied "mockingly" to the modern, egregiously non-epical subject.

Again, as in the case of mock-epic descriptions, the mock-epic plot serves not only as a directly reductive satiric device, but also as a means of realizing the "scene" of mock-epic satire. But the scene that the fable and descriptions of the mock-epic combine to create is hardly what could be called representational. At the very least we have an elaborately heightened or heroic representation of people and manners, such that the relationship between the real world and the world of the poem is highly oblique.

Sometimes the relationship is simply broken, and the poet writes about an imaginary world. Shadwell is real, but the action of *Mac Flecknoe* is not; Belinda's dressing table and Hampton Court Palace are real, but the Sylphs and the Cave of Spleen are not. Within the poems, however, there are no such distinctions. To say that the satirist describes a certain scene in the mock-epic may also mean that he is imaginarily envisioning it; and the scene is presented and taken less as a mirror of society, a catching of the manners living, than as a symbolic exemplification of moral reality.

If we compare the *Dunciad* to *Mac Flecknoe* in this respect, it would seem that the fable and descriptions of the *Dunciad* are more completely given over to the purposes of symbolic expression. Most obviously, Pope makes a pointedly symbolic change in the action of the poem, turning it from satire into prophecy. And while the heroic narrative style in *Mac Flecknoe* is designed mainly to make the subject seem little, in Book 4 of the *Dunciad* it actually, not ironically, enlarges the subject and makes it threatening. At the end of this poem the "mock" of mock-epic is somehow lost; or it is "mock" only in the sense of being "made up"—perhaps "nightmare-epic" would be a better term.

In the *Dunciad*, the qualities we would identify as representational are important only insofar as they embody a satiric or moral meaning. As in so much Augustan satire, the description of the scene is a "seeing" of it in its moral aspect—however fantastic or unnatural the description may be in physical terms.

The impersonal or public manner of speaking that characterizes the satire of Butler, Dryden, Pope, and Johnson and that creates the effect of a generalized and "public" point of view, seems to proceed from the assumption on the part of these writers that reality is most properly defined in moral terms. The assumption is apparent, for instance, in comparing the moral sense in which the Augustan poets use the word "Nature" to the physical sense in which the Romantic poets use it. For the Augustans, the moral nature of things permanent is publicly accessible, something all of us can "see" and concur in seeing just as manifestly as we see rivers and trees. Hence when the Augustan poet describes Nature (as he understands the term), there is no need to call attention to his individual point of view, since it is after all no different—assuming the clarity of his perceptions—from anyone else's.

In later eighteenth-century satire, on the contrary, there is a stronger sense of individual point of view, of the separation of the physical order of reality from the moral. More specifically, we often find an explicit distinction between "seeing" and moralizing, between describing something and expressing an opinion. One sees this awareness in a lefthanded sort of way in Churchill's satirical portrait of Johnson in *The Ghost*, where one of Churchill's complaints about Johnson (or "Pomposo," as he calls him) is that he is always representing as universally apparent that which is after all only personal opinion: "For 'tis with *him* a certain rule, / The Folly's prov'd, when he calls Fool . . ." (bk. 2, ll. 671–72).

As far as the imagery and descriptions of post–Augustan satire are concerned, the distinction makes itself felt in several ways. For example, it occasionally happens that imagery in a satire does not really have a satiric effect, and the use of it cannot clearly be referred to a controlling context, neither amplifying the ridicule nor adding to the scene in the way of symbolic visual furnishings. Many of the descriptive passages in Richard Owen Cambridge's *Scribleriad* fall into this category.

This elaborate attempt at a "pure" mock-epic satire is conceived, as he tells us in his preface, as a satire on false science; but the mock-hero Scriblerus also travels a great deal, and while his pedantic curiosity about out-of-the-way phenomena is represented as foolish, he is allowed to describe them so extensively that we lose all sense of the point. Cambridge wants to represent Scriblerus's pedantry very realistically—to reproduce it, in fact, but in this faithfulness and exactitude leaves satire behind. The implications of his attitude are clear enough at one point in his preface, when he says:

> Such ornaments as were not foreign to my design I have introduced as often as I found a place for them. Of this kind are such particulars in

art or nature as are not commonly known. Thus I have taken an occasion, in describing the Cave of Rumour, to give an exact representation of the famous Latomiae, and of a no less surprising phenomenon in nature, by giving the Surinam toad for one of the prizes.[12]

Here, then, we have satire in which physically accurate description is to some extent a point—one which is inevitably at odds with the purposes of satire.

Thomas Warton, Jr.'s poem *Newmarket* (1751) is subtitled "A Satire" and is intended to be an attack on spendthrift heirs and the fashion of horse racing. When the foolish young Hilario finally inherits his father's estate, Warton gives a "view" of the park and woods of the estate which has little or nothing to do with the poem as satire:

> Behold the Youth with new-felt rapture mark
> Each pleasing prospect of the spacious park
>
> . . . . . . . . . . . . .
>
> Here aged oaks uprear their branches hoar,
> And form dark groves, which Druids might adore;
> With meeting boughs, and deepening to the view,
> Here shoots the broad umbrageous avenue:
> Here various trees compose a chequer'd scene,
> Glowing in gay diversities of green:
> There the full stream thro' intermingling glades
> Shines a broad lake, or falls in deep cascades.[13]

This kind of description is "pure" in the sense that it seems to have no moral implications—is not, as in Pope, a "seeing" that is both visual and conceptual. One has only to compare it to one of Pope's moralized descriptions, where the language appeals now to the eye and now to the mind, to understand the difference. Here is a "scene" in the gardens at Timon's Villa:

> The suff'ring eye inverted Nature sees,
> Trees cut to Statues, Statues thick as trees,
> With here a Fountain, never to be play'd,
> And there a Summer-house, that knows no shade . . .
>
> [*Epistle to Burlington*, ll. 119–22]

Or consider the first stanza of Burns's *The Holy Fair*:

> Upon a simmer Sunday morn,
>> When Nature's face is fair,
> I walked forth to view the corn,
>> An' sniff the caller air.
> The rising sun owre Galston muirs
>> Wi' glorious light was glinting;
> The hares were hirplin down the furrs,
>> The lav'rocks they were chantin
>>> Fu' sweet that day.

This could be the beginning of almost any kind of poem except (one would think) a satire. It seems in these cases that pictorial description has to some extent detached itself from satire and taken on an independent status; and that it is being indulged for its own sake.

Such functionally nonsatiric passages of description do not occur regularly in post–Augustan satire. But they do occur often enough to be noticeable and to add some weight to the idea that the role of imagery and descriptions in the satire of this period is not so carefully subordinate as it is in Augustan satire.

Not that the traditional use of imagery for the sake of a satiric effect is suddenly discontinued. Peter Pindar, for instance, is something of a wizard with the satiric simile:

> Again of Secker boiled th'internal man;
> Thought urging thought, again to rage began:
> Huge thoughts of different sizes swelled his soul;
> Now mounting high, now sinking low, they roll;
> Bustling here, there, up, down, and round about;
> So wild the mob, so terrible the rout.
> How like a Leg of Mutton in the pot,
> With Turnips thick surrounded all so hot!
> Amid the Gulf of Broth, sublime, profound,
> Tumultuous, jostling, how they rush around!
> Now up the Turnips mount with skins of snow,
> While restless labouring Mutton dives below:
> Now lofty soaring climbs the Leg of Sheep,
> Strange such resemblances in things should lie!
> But what escapes the Poet's piercing eye? [14]

But even here there are important differences to be noted. The effect being sought, for one thing, is one of absurd humor more than of satire. The simile is also interesting simply as an inflated description of the "look" of the boiling pot and is presented to us quite selfconsciously (as the last two lines of the quotation show). In fact the poet had already advertised the simile in the "Argument" of the canto in which it appears, referring to it as "One of the finest Comparisons in the World, between Mister Secker in a Passion, and a Leg of Mutton and Turnips in the Pot."

Satiric analogies during the later eighteenth century draw frequently on original contemporary material. This is of course somewhat different from the Augustan satirist's habit of basing his analogies on traditional or otherwise well-conventionalized types of material. It results in more of a double focus, as in the Peter Pindar simile above, where one is not certain whether the homely comparison does not draw more attention to itself as a glimpsed detail of kitchen affairs than it does to Mr. Secker's rage, the thing it is supposed to hit off. Or this from Robert Lloyd's satire *The Poetry Professors* (1762):

> What hunting, changing, toiling, sweating,
> To bring the useful epithet in!
> Where the crampt measure kindly shows
> It *will* be verse, but *should* be prose.
> So, when its neither light nor dark,
> To 'prentice spruce, or lawyer's clerk,
> The nymph, who takes her nightly stand
> At some sly corner in the Strand,
> Plump in the chest, tight in the boddice,
> Seems to the eye a perfect goddess;
> But canvass'd more minutely o'er,
> Turns out an old, stale, batter'd whore.[15]

The analogy is a rather awkward one to begin with, and it loses something more (as a satiric analogy) to the realistic social content of its vehicle. At any rate, the illustrative connection between the satire and the anecdote tends to vanish.

Insofar as it is possible to generalize about the "scene" of Augustan satire as a whole, the illustrative material drawn from external nature or the social life of the time is usually "contained" as to effect. This is a representation of reality as it expresses moral meaning, and as such it "gives us back the image of our mind" and not an image of external nature or social life. Such a scene is probably best characterized as a fusion of appearances and ideas, to which a distinction between "concrete" and "abstract" or "real" and "imaginary" is not especially applicable.

What then is different about the scene of post–Augustan satire? In effect, appearances and ideas break apart. Sometimes it seems almost as if one drives out the other. In some of the satire of the midcentury period—in Whitehead, Churchill, and Chatterton—and again in the conservative satire of Gifford and the *Anti-Jacobin* writers at the end of the century, the scene is virtually divested of a realistic appearance and we are made at the same time more aware of the declamatory effect of the satirist's "voice." In one sense, of course, Churchill and the authors of *New Morality* do describe a scene; but it is an imaginary landscape peopled with personified abstractions. In Churchill, particularly, personification stands as the main illustrative device of the satire. And where Dryden or Pope often introduce material drawn from external reality and describe it in a manner that calls attention simultaneously to its existence *in* reality and its meaning in abstract terms, Churchill's tendency is to substitute abstractions for the material of reality (which he may then describe in such a way as to make them seem to have an existence in reality).

This distinction implies for one thing an attempt to continue to represent reality as capable of being described in generalized moral terms during a period in which that habit of mind is clearly losing ground. In fact it seems likely enough that at such a time a writer might be found explicitly insisting on the "reality" of moral abstractions. We see in Churchill and some of the other satirists of the later century an upsetting of the Augustan balance between the concrete and abstract representation of reality. Churchill, like the Augustans, commands his scene from a "public" or comprehensive point of view, although it might be said that he finds it necessary to write about an imaginary scene in order to maintain this comprehensiveness. His satire is less realistic (in the sense of novel realism) even than Augustan satire.

In other satire of the period the balance is upset in the opposite direction, toward a more concrete representation of reality, one which is also less immediately expressive of a certain meaning. Take for example this scene from Letter 13 of the *New Bath Guide*:

> He said it would greatly our pleasure promote,
> If we all for *Spring-Gardens* set out in a boat:
> I never as yet could his reason explain,
> Why we all sallied forth in the wind and the rain;
> For sure, such confusion was never yet known;
> Here a cap and a hat, there a cardinal blown:
> While his Lordship, embroider'd and powder'd all o'er,
> Was bowing, and handing the ladies a-shore:
> How the misses did huddle and scuddle, and run:
> One would think to be wet must be very good fun;
> For by wagging their tails, they all seem'd to take pains
> To moisten their pinions like ducks when it rains . . .[16]

The moral or satiric context in which these descriptions are embedded is very slight, and it would be hard to say they serve to illustrate a point. It is the appearance of the scene that is principally being emphasized, and the comic effect is produced in visual terms.

Peter Pindar's satire comprises a great deal of anecdote and story, the content of which is almost always contemporary and "realistic." In representing a scene he draws our attention mainly to its external surface, with the result that its satiric meaning (in abstract terms) is largely a matter of inference. *The Churchwarden* (1792) describes how a group of parish officers meet for dinner at a tavern and afterwards, when the time comes to pay, blackmail the innkeeper out of the price of the dinner and twenty pounds besides, by pretending that one of his ex-servant girls has told them she is pregnant by him. I am not suggesting that the satiric meaning of this story is at all difficult to infer, but only that it is an illustration which is not explicitly referred to a meaning; and the author's interest is not by any means "purely" illustrative but to some degree "purely" representational.

Peter is especially interested in striking a picture of the credulous and ingratiating landlord:

> I say, when all were cramm'd unto the chin,
> And every one with wine had fill'd his skin,
> In came the Landlord with a Cherub-smile:
> Around to every one he lowly bow'd;
> Was *vastly happy, honour'd, vastly proud.*
> And then he bow'd again, in *such* a style!
>
> "Hoped *gemmen* liked the dinner, and the wine."—
> To whom the *gemmen* answer'd, "Very fine!
> "A glorious dinner, Larder, to be sure."—
> To which the Landlord, laden deep with bliss,
> Did with his bows so humble almost kiss
>                   The floor.[17]

The *Lousiad,* Peter's mock-epic about the consequences of the King's discovery of a louse on his dinner plate, shows a similar lack of strict satiric "control" over character and scene. At one point in Canto 4, Secker, the Clerk of the Kitchen (whom we have already encountered), enters the kitchen to have the cooks shaved according to the King's command, and the wife of one of the cooks accosts him verbally in a masterpiece of ragtag republicanism:

> "Thomas, I say, shan't lose his Locks, poor dear.—
> Shaved too, 'cause people happen to be *poor*!
> I never heard of such a trick before.
> *Folks* think they may take freedoms with a Cook:
> Go, ask your Master if he'd shave a *Duke*.
> No; if he dared to do it, I'll be curst:
> No, Secker, he would eat the Razor first.
> Good Lord, to think *poor* people's Heads to plunder!
> Why, Lord; are people drunk, or mad, I wonder?
> Because *a* han't Ten Millions in the Stocks?
> Because on me, forsooth, *a* can't bestow
> A Diamond Petticoat, to make a show?
> Marry come up, indeed; a pretty joke!
> Any thing's good enough for humble folk:
> Shoved here and there, forsooth; called Dog and Bitch

(God bless us well!) because we are not rich.
People will soon be beat about with sticks,
Forsooth, because they hadn't a coach and six . . ."[18]

There is satire here, naturally, but one notices too how strongly the
character's point of view is kept and how completely she herself, as
a character sympathetically portrayed, is the focus of the scene. She
is really the satirist in this scene, and it is important to note that the
communication of satiric meaning is conditioned on this woman's
having been convincingly realized as a character. Gratuitous touches
like the "(God bless us well!)" would seem to belong more to the
manner of the novel than to satire.[19]

A more realistic manner of character presentation appears in later
eighteenth-century satire by way of what at first seems to be a return
to the self-incriminating soliloquies of the seventeenth century. But
while those are strictly satiric devices, in which the villain is made to
appear inconsistent as a character in order to deliver certain satiric
charges against himself, in the later instances we find a consistency in
the representation of the character who is speaking, together with a
considerable interest in his motives—something that is never true
in the seventeenth-century examples. Sir Charles Hanbury Williams
imagines a remorseful Pulteney speaking in *An Ode from the Earl of
Bath to Ambition* (ca. 1743):

> Away, Ambition, let me rest;
> All party rage forsake my breast,
>     And opposition cease.
> Arm me no more for future strife,
> Pity my poor remains of life,
>     And give my age its peace.
>
> I'm not the man you knew before,
> For I am Pult'ney now no more,
>     My titles hide my name.
> (Oh, how I blush to own my case!)
> My dignity was my disgrace,
>     And I was rais'd to shame.
>
> To thee I sacrific'd my youth,
> Gave up my honour, friendship, truth,

My king and country's weal.
For thee I sinn'd against my reason,
The daily lie, the weekly treason,
Proclaim'd my blinded zeal.[20]

And on it goes, Pulteney appearing as a figure less of ridicule than of pity. Some of the language of satire remains, as "the daily lie, the weekly treason," but we are prepared by the dramatic context of repentance to accept these words from Pulteney's mouth as possibly being consistent: having recognized his former "blinded zeal," he might very well speak, realistically, of his past as lie and treason.

The most brilliant example of this kind of satire is *Holy Willie's Prayer*, where the adoption of Willie's point of view has the effect of ruling out or at least confusing most of the usual satiric responses of laughter, contempt, disgust, in favor of something more like horrified recognition. The revealed hypocrisy, one feels, is "too real," no doubt in part because of the intimate terms on which Willie is presented to us as a man.

In *Holy Willie's Prayer* and the other similar examples, there is no speaker apparent—no one who explicitly points to the scene or character being represented and calls our attention to it as an illustration of his meaning. In that sense the illustrative material takes in the whole poem, or to put it in more up-to-date terms, the speaker has "withdrawn." There are also instances in the satire of the period in which the declarative voice of the speaker alternates with the representation of scenes and characters. In this case the relationship between declaration and representation is not quite the same as in Augustan satire, where the two are either combined in a single expression or the representation is a strongly stylized or otherwise well-"contained" illustration of the declared meaning. Instead, the representation may be considerably more realistic, more clearly conceived in its own right as representation, such that the speaker's declaration of meaning takes the form of a commentary on what he is representing, an interpretation of this particular bit of "reality." That which is abstract (the speaker's thoughts) seems, once again, definitely distinct from that which is concrete (the represented scene).

Cowper, for example, has a characteristic of picturing a certain scene and then interpreting it to the reader. The effect is to emphasize point of view, as though "scene" were one thing and "meaning-of-the scene" were another. In the satirical passage on gypsies in *The Task*, Cowper first evokes the scene of the gypsies' camp, visually, and then works from that into his satirical ideas:

I see a column of slow rising smoke
O'ertop the lofty wood that skirts the wild.
A vagabond and useless tribe there eat
Their miserable meal. A kettle, slung
Between two poles upon a stick transverse,
Receives the morsel—flesh obscene of dog,
Or vermin, or, at best, of cock purloin'd
From his accustom'd perch. Hard faring race!
They pick their fuel out of ev'ry hedge,
Which, kindled with dry leaves, just saves unquench'd
The spark of life. The sportive wind blows wide
Their flutt'ring rags, and shows a tawny skin,
The vellum of the pedigree they claim.
Great skill have they in palmistry, and more
To conjure clean away the gold they touch,
Conveying worthless dross into its place;
Loud when they beg, dumb only when they steal.

[bk. 1, ll. 557–73]

Here it is clear that seeing something and expressing thoughts about it are two different things, and Cowper shows a certain respect for the physical appearance of reality quite apart from whatever moral significance it may have. This distinction between the physical and moral dimension of reality, the objective and subjective, is especially emphasized at the beginning of *Expostulation*, where Cowper deliberately plays up the difficulty of extracting the proper meaning from the given reality of the physical scene in England's "delightful isle":

Why weeps the Muse for England? What appears
In England's case to move the muse to tears?
From side to side of her delightful isle,
Is she not cloth'd with a perpetual smile?
Can nature add a charm, or art confer

A new-found luxury, not seen in her?
Where under heav'n is pleasure more pursued?
Or where does cold reflection less intrude?
Her fields a rich expanse of wavy corn,
Pour'd out from plenty's overflowing horn ...

[ll. 1–10]

In Byron the distinction is felt even more positively than in Cowper, although of course the content of the scenes and commentary is entirely different. Particularly in *Don Juan*, one is always made aware (by Byron himself) of the story as against the personal reflections which are more or less prompted by it: Byron the narrator versus Byron the speaker.[21] In many ways, of course, *Don Juan* by its comprehensiveness and its frequently satirical intentions would seem to invite comparison with the Augustan mock-epic satires. But besides the more obvious differences in tone and procedure there is the matter of point of view: Dryden and Pope write so as to efface or exclude any sense of an individual point of view (except occasionally, as at the end of the *Dunciad*), whereas Byron not only allows this but also exploits it. Hence in Byron the characteristic separation of "narrator" and "speaker," "scene" and "commentary," which is not apparent in Dryden and Pope and which implies that external reality, on the one hand, and the individual point of view, on the other, each have an independently privileged existence. *Don Juan* may be (and indeed has been) thought of as a "realistic" poem; something it is hard to imagine being said of *Absalom and Achitophel* or the *Dunciad*.

## CHAPTER 5

# Irony and Invective

THE WORD "irony" in this chapter is meant to be taken in its familiar sense as signifying a certain method of expressing meaning, in which the speaker or writer more or less consistently says the opposite of what he actually means. When a satirist adopts the ironical mode of writing, he is essentially making an extended adaptation of one or more of the classical ironic tropes—*ironia, meiosis, litotes*—by which he misrepresents his true feelings at the level of literal statement in order to be understood only indirectly, thus to bring about any of the various characteristic effects that are associated with this mode of satire.

Irony has an extraliterary dimension of meaning in that it can also be considered as a certain mode of behavior. In this broadest possible sense, irony is a directly personal characteristic, a temperamental expression of the man rather than a formal quality of the work. Northrop Frye points out how this is the conception of irony in Aristotle's *Ethics,* "where the *eiron* is the man who deprecates himself, as opposed to the *alazon.* Such a man makes himself invulnerable, and, though Aristotle disapproves of him, there is no question that he is a predestined artist, just as the *alazon* is one of his predestined victims." Frye goes on to define irony as behavior that sometimes manifests itself as a literary technique:

> The term irony, then, indicates a technique of appearing to be less than one is, which in literature becomes most commonly a technique of saying as little and meaning as much as possible, or, in a more general way,

a pattern of words that turns away from direct statement or its own obvious meaning.[1]

The opposite of the ironic mode is invective, in which the author does all he can to express or indeed to exaggerate his true feelings. Invective, like irony, has a rhetorical basis, as in the various metaphors by which the satirist might turn his enemies into pigs and asses. And this mode too has the effect of imputing a certain personality to the author: the man who writes invective is righteously indignant, too honest to keep from speaking out, or perhaps malicious (depending on how carefully he tries to avoid this particular imputation).

One thinks of irony as a more sophisticated phase of satire than invective. Oldham's *Satires upon the Jesuits* are more direct, hence less subtle, than Pope's *Epistle to Augustus*. And the same thing is generally true of most late seventeenth-century satire (e.g., the *Poems on Affairs of State*), when compared to the ironic satire that Pope and Swift brought to perfection. But here a distinction should be made between what the satirist actually says about the object of his ridicule and the context in which he says it. He may (unironically) say what he means in an (ironically) inappropriate context. Such is the case in forms like the "instructions to a painter," the parody litany, or the mock heroic, in which the relation between form and content is ironic even though the content itself consists only of direct abuse. Likewise the parodic imitation of satiric characters, as in Rochester's *Tunbridge-Wells*, constitutes irony as distinct from the unironic manner in which the narrator may ridicule the same characters. More will be said about this in connection with *Mac Flecknoe*.

Commonwealth and Restoration satire owes a debt to the Renaissance concept of the satyr, whose mode of speaking is directly abusive ("sharpe") rather than ironic. There is very little indirectness, for example, in the *Rump Songs* (1662), the collection of satirical poems and ballads written between 1639 and 1661 against Cromwell and the Commonwealth. The *O tempora* theme is a favorite starting point for many of these writers: England under Cromwell is "A Mad World my Masters."[2] The satiric reaction to this situation is almost always direct, taking one of two characteristic forms: either a sentimental longing for the old, lost values, or a denunciation of the new ones. In

*The Penitent Traytor* the author sorrowfully complains that loyalty and wisdom have become crimes. Symbolizing the new values are the Roundhead and his "Rump Rampant," who together invite a simple, occasionally hysterical kind of invective aimed at exaggerating their vices enormously.[3]

The great object of scorn and bitterness in the *Rump Songs*—the deposition and execution of Charles—is also what opened up the very possibility of this kind of political satire. By the time Charles II came to the throne, monarchical rule itself had become a partisan affair, something to be defended or attacked, apologized for or satirized. This was also, as James Sutherland says, "one of the golden periods of English invective."[4] Its great memorial is the *Poems on Affairs of State*, which is a revealing catalogue of most of the satiric possibilities of the mode of invective. These poems often consist of a series of abusive observations on particular individuals and situations, each of them relatively independent of the other. The result is a sequential or "episodic" satire in which multiple meaning is at a minimum. Take for example this anonymous Juvenalian imitation of 1680, entitled *Satire*:

> Must I with patience ever silent sit,
> Perplex'd with fools who will believe they've wit?
> Must I find ev'ry place by coxcombs seiz'd,
> Hear their affected nonsense and seem pleas'd?
> Must I meet Heveningham where'er I go,
> Arp, Arran, villain Frank, nay Poulteney too?
> Shall Hewitt pertly crawl from place to place,
> And scabby Villiers for a beauty pass?
> Shall Howe and Brandon politicians prove,
> And Sutherland presume to be in love?
> Shall pimping Deincourt patient cuckolds blame,
> Lumley and Savage against Pope declaim?
> Who can abstain from satire in this age?
> What nature wants I find suppli'd by rage.[5]

The combination of a very weak, repetitive principle of structure ("and . . . and . . .") with purely derogatory epithets ("villain," "scabby," "pimping") is characteristic of many of the *Poems on Affairs of State*.

The mode in which the satirist externalizes his feelings—invective—requires him to represent those feelings directly, as they truly are; or at least he must, as a matter of convention, seem to be doing this.

Ironic ridicule in Restoration satire is usually a short-lived departure from the habitual mode of invective. That is, irony may be a limited rhetorical device (i.e., blame by praise) which the satirist occasionally uses to relieve the directness of his attack; it is not, however, the mode of the satiric work, the "policy" or controlling principle in terms of which every judgment that the satirist makes must be interpreted. One of the *Poems on Affairs of State* promises by its title and first few lines to satisfy this definition of the ironic mode: this is *An Ironical Satire* (1680), which begins with the obviously false proposition that

> Not Rome in all her splendor could compare
> With these great blessings happy Britons share.
> Vainly they boast their kings of heav'nly race:
> A god incarnate England's throne does grace.
> Chaste in his pleasures, in devotion grave,
> To his friends constant, to his foes he's brave;
> His justice is through all the world admir'd,
> His word held sacred, and his scepter fear'd.
>
> [ll. 1–8]

But the author neglects to insist on the ironic premise, and what began as mock-encomium dissolves formlessly into the more usual tedious namecalling:

> Then for commanders both by sea and land,
> Heav'n has bestow'd 'em with a liberal hand.
> York, who thrice chang'd his ship through warlike rage,
> And Mulgrave, who's the Scipio of the age.
> The first long admiral, but more renown'd
> For pox and Popery than public wound:
> This is the man whose vice each satire feeds,
> And for whom no one virtue intercedes;
> Destin'd for England's plague from infant time,
> Curs'd with a person fouler than his crime.[6]

This example, and others like it,[7] suggest that the typical Restoration satirist did not think of irony as a general mode of satire, but instead as a specific verbal device. This relatively restricted concept of irony, as Norman Knox shows,[8] was inherited from Renaissance dictionaries and manuals of rhetoric, in which the classical definition of irony as a figure of speech dominated. And in the absence of any need to enlarge the inherited meaning to account for cases, it lingers on until early in the eighteenth century.

The Restoration writers do not offer much in the way of a theory of satire, but what theory there is assumes that the basic method of attacking someone is to call him a bad name. Certainly this idea is justified by the actual practice of Restoration satirists, whose favorite genre is unquestionably the lampoon or "libel." But Dryden, reacting against the witless abuse he finds in most lampooning satire, calls for subtlety and indirection instead, as in the famous passage on "fine raillery" in the *Discourse concerning Satire*:

> How easy is it to call rogue and villain, and that wittily! But how hard to make a man appear a fool, a blockhead, or a knave, without using any of those opprobrious terms! To spare the grossness of the names, and to do the thing yet more severely, is to draw a full face, and to make the nose and cheeks stand out, and yet not to employ any depth of shadowing. This is the mystery of that noble trade, which yet no master can teach to his apprentice . . .[9]

To illustrate his ideal of a stylistically subtle and "witty" ridicule, Dryden points to his portrait of Zimri in *Absalom and Achitophel*. Granted that the names he calls Buckingham are not especially "opprobrious" compared to what one of the "common lampooners" might have called him, but even so, the basic strategy of direct abuse—name-calling, in other words—is no different.

Dryden's idealized satiric formula, with its emphasis on wit, logically would lead in the direction of irony. Dryden tells the satirist to refine the quality of his abuse, which would mean, ultimately, making abuse sound like praise. Dryden himself does this in his satires, but only in a qualified sense. *Mac Flecknoe*, for example, illustrates how the two modes of invective and irony can operate in a satire at the same time. One controls what Dryden says, the other controls the way he says it. The poem is built on an ironic premise, which is that Dulness should be treated heroically. Once this premise is allowed, the style of the poem becomes mock-heroic, the hero becomes a mock hero, and the scale of values seems to turn upside down. Actually these values are never really inverted, since the poet continues to call dunces the people who really are dunces. But as Ian Jack puts it, "the heroic idiom is continually asserting that the hero is a great man," even though he is always *called* a fool.[10] Dryden says what he means in a manner he does not mean.

The irony of *Mac Flecknoe* is formal: explicitly stated ridicule set in a conventional laudatory form. But in a more pervasively ironic satire, the satirist himself changes character, playing a role that in every respect falsifies his real attitude. Needless to say, this definition of the ironic mode is an idealized one, for in fact only a relatively few satires of the Restoration and eighteenth-century period satisfy it, although among them are some of the most memorable works of the period, such as the *Modest Proposal*. Pope's irony, for example, most frequently falls into the same category as the irony of *Mac Flecknoe*, in that he normally *says* what he more or less means; but this is putting a strict construction on it, because in a more general sense it is obvious that Pope habitually puts a certain face on his ridicule, i.e., heroic, tragic, Horatian, which makes it much less directly expressive than simple name-calling. And in the literature of the Pope–Swift circle generally, most obviously in Swift, there is clearly a much stronger tendency in favor of ironic methods of satire than there is among the Restoration satirists taken as a whole.

The question of why this should have been so is worth trying to answer. Swift tells us that he "was born to introduce" irony, that he "refin'd it first, and shew'd its Use."[11] Swift's irony, according to Ian Watt, is a defensive reaction against the "mob": as a member of the "elite," a "righteous minority," Swift is conscious of "a divided audience which made irony, in the sense of speaking by contraries, a possible, and almost an obligatory mode of discourse."[12] The Scriblerus Club elite, then, are descended in a sense from the true wits of the Restoration stage, who likewise ridicule or "smoke" the false wits, the pretenders to the club, in a style of mock-sincerity that goes over their heads and is understood only by the other members of the club. In the intensity of this common effort to defend against the mob, to put it in Watt's terms, the satirist is willing to relinquish the direct expression of his own personality and attitudes to some extent, as he must if he is to adopt the ironic code speech of the special group to which he belongs. But we should also consider that the most singularly successful example of this ironic self-falsification, Defoe's *Shortest Way with the Dissenters*, is something of a failure as satire because Defoe hides his true feelings well enough to keep anybody from sensing the irony.[13] Poor Defoe has to be his own audience, chagrined and even desperate, but certainly not amused.

Swift having "showed the use" of irony, the accepted meaning of that word broadened considerably during the first half of the eighteenth century. Between 1720 and 1730, according to Knox, the word "settled into literary discussion and general speech as one of the conventional terms of literary reference."[14] At first the popular definition clearly lagged behind the practice of irony, as if, one might say, it took the mob a little time to discover what was the weapon being used against them. But eventually the meaning broadens, in the sense that it comes to include "irony of manner," as it has sometimes been called.[15] In the *Remarks on the Life and Writings of Dr. Jonathan Swift* (1752), for instance, Lord Orrery is able to speak familiarly of the manner in which Swift likes to "smile under his usual mask of gravity."[16]

But by Orrery's time theory had also virtually overtaken practice. Since the concept of the ironic mode was well known, most readers had no trouble recognizing it or grasping the intent of a wholly ironic satire; but neither did they have much occasion to. For if Pope and Swift exhibit a tendency toward ironic, mocking, or otherwise roundabout modes of expressing ridicule, there is in post–Augustan satire an equally strong tendency toward direct expression.

For many of these satirists, such as Churchill, "*Self*" is "that darling, luscious theme,"[17] and of course this is the theme for which the ironic mode is perhaps worst suited. There is great satiric power in the mask of irony, but in terms of midcentury values the price of writing ironically seems to have gone too high. As Fielding observes in the *Jacobite's Journal* for 26 March 1748 (in which he publicly drops the pose of a Jacobite), irony involves the impersonation of someone you detest; and "tho' Irony is capable of furnishing the most exquisite Ridicule; yet as there is no kind of Humour so liable to be mistaken, it is, of all others, the most dangerous to the Writer. An infinite Number of Readers have not the least Taste or Relish for it, I believe I may say do not understand it; and all are apt to be tired, when it is carried to any Degree of Length."[18]

### IRONY AND INVECTIVE: CHURCHILL

Fielding drops his pose in the *Jacobite's Journal* partly because he does not like pretending to be a Jacobite, but mainly because he thinks the pretense may confuse his audience. He *can* write ironically but decides not to. It appears that Churchill, on the other hand, sometimes decides to write ironically but finds it difficult to keep up the necessary pretense. He seems to have admired Swift,[19] and in a more general way, he inherited a tradition of irony in such well-established types as the mock heroic and ironic eulogy. But Churchill's irony is inconsistent: Swift would have said, as he did say of an earlier would-be ironist, that "the author . . . has not continued the irony to the end."[20]

Churchill, of course, is chiefly famous (even in his own day) for a vigorous, if anachronistic, type of invective, and in that respect it is not really fair to discuss him as an ironist, or a would-be ironist— something he clearly was never in the main trying to be. Yet he does occasionally adopt this mode, and I think that the inconsistency with which he treats it is not so much a case of artistic clumsiness as it is a reflection of the artistic importance he assigns to the idea of the *honnête homme* and to the principle of independent self-expression. By way of making a fuller explanation of this point, then, I shall concentrate on three of his poems in which the relationship between the two modes of irony and invective is especially revealing: the *Rosciad*, the *Prophecy of Famine*, and the unfinished *Dedication to Warburton* that was prefixed to the volume of Churchill's sermons posthumously published in 1765.

### *"The Rosciad"*

Dryden says that "the word satire is of more general signification in Latin, than in French, or English. For amongst the Romans it was not only used for those discourses which decried vice, or exposed folly, but for others also, where virtue was recommended."[21] Maynard Mack is thinking of the same thing when he says that "rhetorically considered, satire belongs to the category of *laus et vituperatio*, praise and blame."[22] The English satirist may typically make conventional allusions to his satire in somewhat similar terms, as though to indicate that he is as interested in recommending virtue as in decrying vice. But it is a meaningless protest, a gesture perhaps in the interest of improving the satirist's credibility but obviously not an accurate description of his satire itself. Thus we hear Dryden regretting that in England the word "satire" has lost its more "general signification" and has become synonymous merely with invective, all blame and no praise.[23]

Churchill in the *Rosciad* also makes this familiar profession that he is as anxious to praise as he is to blame, but in his particular instance we are dealing with something more than a merely conventional gesture. Here is a poem that has some of the appearances of ironic satire—a kind of mock-epic—but which finally is not ironic. The motto on the title page reads:

> Unknowing, and unknown, the hardy Muse
> Boldly defies all mean and partial Views:
> With honest Freedom plays the Critic's Part,
> And praises, as she censures, from the Heart.

Actors and acting are the subject of the poem; the object is to play the critic's part; the mode, significantly, is to be an unblinking directness of expression, indeed a speaking from the heart. Despite the suggestive "-iad" tag and some other such superficial resemblances, then, the *Rosciad* is not a mock-heroic poem at all. Its scale of values is thoroughly right side up, and the stylistic machinery, when it is brought into service, is not meant ironically to confuse those values. The style, that is, does not seem to say the actors are something they are not. Instead it says what they are, bad or good, strictly according to the announced intention of the motto.

The narrative content of the poem is very slight, and there is little in the way of an "action." This element is comprehended by the first two lines: "ROSCIUS deceas'd, each high aspiring play'r / Push'd all his int'rest for the vacant chair." Roscius is no "type" of the bad actor, as Dryden's Flecknoe is of the bad poet. Soon after the death of the historical Roscius, of course, his name was being applied generically to talented Roman actors. His "vacant chair," then, is a desirable goal on the real scale of values as well as the scale projected in the poem: the two scales, that is, are identical.

The question Churchill raises is how to "form our judgment." "What can an actor give?" he asks, applying himself almost sympathetically to the problem that actors "can't, like candidate for other seat, / Pour seas of wine, and mountains raise of meat" (ll. 23–24). The Town, Churchill says, has a way of forming judgment, but it is the wrong way: they decide "as passion, humour, int'rest, party, sways" (l. 38). On this reductive basis a dwarf will decide that one actor is too tall, while to a six-footer Garrick is too short.

The first of the only two real actions of the poem comes when the actors agree to have the succession settled by "some one judge" (l. 58). Naturally they cannot decide on one, and the subsequent uproar gives Churchill the occasion of censuring (directly) most of the names that arise. Arthur Murphy asks to have the chair itself instead of the job of judge; and in a passage added in the eighth edition, Churchill paints a brutal portrait of Thady Fitzpatrick, "of the Fribble Tribe" (l. 141), who had been the hero of Garrick's *Fribbleriad*. The lines owe something to Pope's Sporus and even more to Garrick's poem, but the "bruising" effect is Churchill's own. It is very well done for what it is, which is one sarcastic innuendo wrought upon and repeated sufficiently to bring the unstated—hence technically ironic—point of ridicule up to a level of the most transparent obviousness:

> Much did *It* talk in its own pretty phrase,
> Of Genius and of Taste, of Play'rs and Plays;
> Much too of writings, which *Itself* had wrote,
> Of special merit, tho' of little note,
> For fate, in a strange humor, had decreed
> That what *It* wrote, none but *Itself* should read;
> Much too *It* chatter'd of *Dramatic* Laws,
> Misjudging Critics, and misplac'd applause,
> Then, with a self-complacent jutting air,

*It smil'd, It smirk'd, It wriggled to the chair;*
And with an awkward briskness not his own,
Looking around, and *perking* on the throne,
Triumphant seem'd, when that strange savage Dame,
Known but to few, or only known by name,
Plain COMMON SENSE appear'd, by Nature there
Appointed, with plain TRUTH, to guard the Chair.
The Pageant saw, and blasted with her frown,
To *Its* first state of Nothing melted down.

[ll. 153–70]

Here the manner in which Churchill ridicules Fitzpatrick is of course directly reductive rather than ironically heroic: Fitzpatrick mounts the throne, but unlike the typical mock hero he is out of place from the very beginning.

With "Fribble" out of the way the poem returns to the problem it began with: Who will judge the players? Now it is the critics' turn, and it is they who precipitate the resolution of the question. Churchill makes a rather pointed connection between their virility and their capacity to judge:[24]

Cold-blooded critics, by enervate sires
Scarce hammer'd out, when nature's feeble fires
Glimmer'd their last; whose sluggish blood, half froze,
Creeps lab'ring thro' the veins; whose heart ne'er glows
With fancy-kindled heat:—A servile race,
Who, in mere want of fault, all merit place;
Who blind obedience pay to ancient schools,
Bigots to Greece, and slaves to musty rules . . .

[ll. 179–86]

The critics then call for Sophocles to be judge, and the crowd, "obsequious to the sacred dictate" (l. 190), goes along with them. But in an amazing turn of events Churchill's friend Robert Lloyd "stemm'd the mighty critic flood" (l. 194) by delivering a speech in favor of the native British judges Shakespeare and Jonson. Thus Lloyd

said, and conquer'd.—Sense resum'd her sway,
And disappointed pedants stalk'd away.

> SHAKESPEAR and JONSON, with deserv'd applause,
> Joint-judges were ordain'd to try the cause.
>
> [ll. 227–30]

Lloyd here is a sort of *deus ex machina*, introduced to sway an audience who by the established terms of the poem itself would never have been swayed by such a speech. Churchill had settled that the crowd was "obsequious" to the critics, and yet Lloyd merely "said, and conquer'd." In the typical satiric "world," where power is frequently seen to be in the hands of the fools and the knaves, such a thing could hardly have happened. But in the *Rosciad* power passes very quickly into the right hands (Shakespeare and Jonson are chosen instead of the critics' "man" Sophocles), and the preparation for a fair trial, then, far from representing the way of the world, is an imaginary fulfillment of the way Churchill would like the world to be—a world, as in *Gotham*, in which proper values take their proper places.

Now that the assize for the actors is about to begin, Churchill again flirts with the idea of the mock heroic, but ends by rejecting it as inappropriate to his purpose:

> Now should I, in some sweet poetic line,
> Offer up incense at APOLLO's shrine;
> Invoke the muse to quit her calm abode,
> And waken mem'ry with a sleeping ode.
> For how should mortal man, in mortal verse,
> Their titles, merits, or their names rehearse?
> But give, kind Dulness, memory and rhime,
> We'll put off Genius till another time.
>
> [ll. 287–94]

These actors, that is, are to be treated as they deserve to be; Churchill's decision to render them "in mortal verse" is of course in keeping with the theme of the fair trial at the hands of a fair-minded pair of judges, the whole show being presented as an exemplary exercise in honest criticism.

At this point Churchill virtually forgets the dramatic premise of an assize in giving over the poem to a catalogue of the merits and demerits of some two dozen contemporary actors and actresses. Here especially, where Churchill has done the most revising and expanding in order to embalm as many of these seasonal curiosities as he can, the poem could be said to contain satire without at the same time qualifying, in its overall conception, as a satire. Every actor is an individual case, requiring individual treatment if the promise of the motto is to be fulfilled.

As the various players troop by to have sentence pronounced, blame outweighs praise, but not by much. Some receive mixed notices, as for example James Quin, the actor of an older school than Garrick's; he scorns acting in the modern style, to which Churchill cautiously replies,

> Far be it from the candid muse to tread
> Insulting o'er the ashes of the dead.
> But, just to living merit, she maintains,
> And dares the test, whilst GARRICK's Genius reigns;
> Ancients, in vain, endeavour to excel,
> Happily prais'd, if they could act as well.
>
> [ll. 933–38]

Here again is the controlling idea of a "candid muse": Churchill gives the verdict in favor of Garrick, but conspicuously shows a sensitive forbearance toward the old actor Quin, and goes on in the next few lines (939–44) to praise him handsomely. Next comes an even more ambiguous case, that of Thomas Sheridan:

> A doubtful name,
> As yet unsettled in the rank of fame.
> This, fondly lavish in his praises grown,
> Gives him all merit; That allows him none.
> Between them both, we'll steer the middle course,
> Nor, loving praise, rob judgment of her force.
>
> [ll. 987–92]

The comparison of the generation past (Quin) with the generation to come (Sheridan) ends in a neat resolution in Garrick, who like the other two is given credit and discredit where they are properly due. The idea here is that Churchill is "a poor dull creature, still with Nature Pleas'd" (l. 1068), and not the oversubtle or partial critic that great performers like Garrick inevitably attract. Garrick enters, for instance, as "behind him throng a train / Of snarling critics, ignorant as vain" (ll. 1027–28)). Churchill cannot overcome all their petty objections to Garrick's acting style, but when he agrees with them he is careful to imply that his judgment has a more substantial basis than theirs; he is, once more, the honest critic with no axes to grind. "I can't acquit by wholesale, nor condemn" (l. 1038).

Churchill chooses Garrick for the chair. Shakespeare is made to deliver the "sentence" to that effect, and it is interesting that his speech is given as a hypothesis:

> 'If manly Sense; if Nature link'd with Art;
> 'If thorough knowledge of the Human Heart;
> 'If Pow'rs of acting vast and unconfined;
> 'If fewest Faults, with greatest Beauties join'd;
> 'If strong Expression, and strange Pow'rs, which lie
> 'Within the magic circle of the Eye;
> 'If feelings which few hearts, like his, can know,
> 'And which no face so well as His can show;
> 'Deserve the Pref'rence;—GARRICK take the Chair;
> 'Nor quit it—'till Thou place an Equal there.'
>
> [ll. 1081–90]

Even here we are made aware of Garrick's assumption of the chair of Roscius as a qualified conquest, and Churchill is clearly concerned to represent this judgment as criticism, not hero-worship: "fewest Faults, with greatest Beauties join'd." The inability to acquit or condemn wholesale, the "middle way," are themes carried through to the last line of the poem, and in that way Churchill invites a comparison between his method, the fair trial, and the usual approach the critics take to their material. The *Rosciad* itself is an exemplum showing how a true critic's judgment should be formed and passed. The poem is not formless by any means, and the actors do fit into the framework Churchill builds—that is, they fit into the proposed exercise in honest criticism. This framework, however, does not grow out of the subject but instead is imposed upon it, so one has the feeling that any subject might have served as well.

This has the effect of leaving us with a poem about two things, or more specifically, two professions: criticism and acting. The particular pose Churchill adopts calls for him to seem to say exactly what he thinks. His praise (Garrick) must be as candid as his blame (Fitzpatrick). Invective is a kind of candid blame—the most candid blame, in fact, since the author as honest critic cannot permit himself to lie about his feelings. But the mixture of praise and blame makes the poem a satire by starts only, unless we should give "satire" the more general Latin sense of which Dryden speaks. The occasional objects of Churchill's ridicule cannot be defined in terms of any one satiric theme; this is because the unifying theme of the poem is how to be a good critic, and that of course is not a ridiculous or ironic matter.

### "The Prophecy of Famine"

The pose that Churchill adopts in the *Rosciad* is congenial to his personality; he does not detest the character he is impersonating, because for one thing he is hardly impersonating a character at all. In the *Prophecy of Famine*, however, we find him occasionally writing in the pretended person of someone he does not like. The poem itself is Churchill's first major political exercise, a dramatized warning to Englishmen that the Scots are preparing to overrun their country. It is also, as he calls it, a "Scots Pastoral," and begins not with politics but instead with some criticism of the pastoral.

His opening attack is a parody of the conventions of this genre:

> Clad, as your nymphs were always clad of yore,
> In rustic weeds—a cook-maid now no more—
> Beneath an aged oak LARDELLA lies—
> Green moss, her couch; her canopy, the skies.
> From aromatic shrubs the *roguish* gale
> Steals *young* perfumes, and wafts them thro' the vale.
> The youth, turn'd swain, and skill'd in rustic lays,
> Fast by her side his am'rous descant plays.
> Herds lowe, Flocks bleat, Pies chatter, Ravens scream,
> And the full chorus dies a-down the stream.
>
> [ll. 15–24]

The first line of this passage gives away Churchill's intentions by hitting at the overfamiliarized material and form of pastoral: "as *your* nymphs were *always* clad of *yore*." Convention implies imitation, which in Churchill's lexicon of values is a type of slavery. We know from other poems, especially the youthful *Epistle to R. L. L.*, that Churchill habitually takes the side of the Moderns; there is a great difference, he tells us, between "an admiring slave" and the true son

> Who when a parent's worth is known,
> Can't rest until it is his own,
> Nor stops, inflam'd with virtue's fire,
> But dares be better than his sire.
>
> [ll. 115–18]

In lines 29–110 of the *Prophecy of Famine* Churchill applies this test to the modern pastoral, where imitation takes the place of genius, and "nature's banish'd by *mechanic* art" (l. 36). The "mechanic" poet models his work "after some *great man*, whose name breeds awe" (l. 31), and as a result

> Trifles are dignified, and taught to wear
> The robes of Ancients with a Modern air,
> NONSENSE with *Classic* ornaments is grac'd,
> And passes current with the stamp of TASTE.
>
> [ll. 43–46]

The poets who ape this formula produce ludicrous anomalies, as when "roses blush, but blush without a thorn" (l. 56). These are "bards" who are all form and no content: ". . . who neither sing nor say, / Grave without thought, and without feeling gay . . ." (ll. 59–60). Churchill himself, on the other hand, is the kind of poet whom "no judgment tempers when rash genius fires" (l. 80), and who is ". . . thus ev'ry way unfit / For *pacing* poesy, and *ambling* wit . . ." (ll. 89–90). Finally come the lines beginning "Thou, Nature, art *my* goddess . . ." (93–110), which also serve to introduce the subject of Scotland. Churchill makes the transition seem logical, since in a "northern clime" like Scotland nature still "reigns throughout the year" and is "undisturb'd by Art's rebellious plan" (ll. 108–9).

This account of the first part of the poem should make it clear that Churchill rather abruptly abandons the ironic pose with which he begins. At first he is the wretched pastoral poet, but soon undermines the irony by surrendering several times to the impulse to remind the reader that he is only pretending, that he of course is not serious. And before long he leaves pretense behind altogether, as he openly expatiates on his objections to the pastoral. Here he goes from a general indictment of imitation as one kind of slavery to increasingly specific topics: the habit of imitating Theocritus and Virgil, the current sad state of English pastoral poetry, and finally, most specific of all, the subject of himself. All this time, of course, the "real" (or unironic) Churchill has been coming into better focus—has, within only fifty lines or so, become the opposite of what he had been pretending to be.

Having broached the subject of Scotland, Churchill turns to his main theme of England's potentially dangerous position with respect to Scotland. Once again, his treatment is at first impersonal and ironic:

> To that rare soil, where virtues clust'ring grow,
> What mighty blessings doth not ENGLAND owe,
> What waggon-loads of courage, wealth and sense,
> Doth each revolving day import from thence?
>
> [ll. 111–14]

Following the ironic assertion that England owes Scotland "mighty blessings," Churchill points in illustration to some fairly harmless Scottish imports, such as "that *old, new, Epic Pastoral,* Fingal" (l. 130) and a host of "simple bards, by simple prudence taught," who "In simple manner utter simple lays, / And take, with simple pensions, simple praise" (ll. 135–38). In these lines Churchill is beginning to sound like himself again. The pressure on the meaning of the word "simple" builds by repetition. When Churchill first uses it, in "simple bards," it means unspoiled or "natural" because his earlier assertion that Scotland harbors nature "undisturb'd" makes us expect that meaning. By continuing to draw attention to the word, however, and applying it each time to a slightly less appropriate noun ("manner . . . lays . . . pensions . . . praise"), Churchill forces it to be taken in another sense. Now it means "simple-minded," which of course is what Churchill actually means to say about these poets.

Following a tribute to John Wilkes (ll. 149–78), Churchill shifts his emphasis from England to Scotland in an attempt to develop a reasonable or, as he would say, a "candid" view of that nation. Still addressing himself to Wilkes, he makes a curious declaration:

> Oft have I heard thee mourn the wretched lot
> Of the poor, mean, despis'd, insulted *Scot*,
> Who, might calm reason credit idle tales,
> By rancour forg'd where prejudice prevails,
> Or starves at home, or practises, thro' fear
> Of starving, arts which damn all conscience here.
> When *Scriblers*, to the charge by int'rest led,
> The fierce *North-Briton* foaming at their head,
> Pour forth invectives, deaf to candour's call,
> And, injur'd by one alien, rail at all;
> On *Northern Pisgah* when they take their stand,
> To mark the weakness of that *Holy Land*,
> With needless truths their libels to adorn,
> And hang a nation up to public scorn,
> Thy gen'rous soul condemns the frantic rage,
> And hates the faithful, but ill-natur'd, page.
>
> [bk. 2, ll. 179–94]

There is no irony here. Churchill, as he has done before, is making large concessions to the (nominal) enemy on behalf of an ideal of candor. The opposite of being candid is being ill-natured, especially at midcentury, and Churchill goes so far as to say that his own journal, the *North Briton*, is not candid in its view of Scotland. Everything he says in this passage is perfectly true: the Scot is indeed "poor, mean, despis'd, insulted," and the English political writers do indeed "hang a nation up to public scorn." If the Scots, "by low supple arts successful grown, /. . . sapp'd our vigour to increase their own" (ll. 199–200), then Reason rightly should mobilize every resource of the English nation, including her writers, against the unjust robbery (ll. 201–4). On the other hand,

> If they revere the hand by which they're fed,
> And bless the donors for their daily bread,
> Or by vast debts of higher import bound,
> Are always humble, always grateful found,
> If they, directed by PAUL's holy pen,

Become discretely all things to all men,
That all men may become all things to them,
Envy may hate, but justice can't condemn.

[ll. 208–14]

All true enough, but Churchill's Pauline definition of a "just Scot" has become too exacting for anyone to fulfill in practical terms; hence the possibility that the Scots are being wronged becomes an ironic possibility. On this cue Churchill jestingly proposes to right the wrong, to "raise new trophies to the Scottish name" (l. 234).

At this point William Whitehead, "Folly's chief friend, Decorum's eldest son" (l. 257), breaks in to tell Churchill that his theme is "too lofty for a bard so mean" (l. 261). The singer of the Scottish eclogue ironically submits, saying "*Discretion* beckons to an humbler scene" (l. 262). This turns out to be the rustic exchange between Jockey and Sawney which, together with the culminating prophecy of Famine, concludes the poem. Thus far in the poem Churchill's personal role has been constantly shifting. First he is the vapid pastoral poet, then is again himself (a hard critic of such poetry and a servant of his goddess Nature); next he pretends to defend Scotland by pointing out all the "blessings" that country has given England; but to this he adds a digressive tribute to Wilkes rendered in his own voice which in fact carries over into the "candid" criticism of the way the Scots are blamed indiscriminately; and finally he returns to the original pose of pastoral poet—whose wretchedness, incidentally, is confirmed by the wretchedly nonidyllic subject he is forced to write about.

Up to now Churchill himself has been the principal "character" in the poem, just as he is in the *Rosciad* and for that matter in most of his poems. When he introduces Jockey and Sawney, however, he becomes primarily a narrator. First there is the description, after Pope, of the cave of Famine:

All creatures, which, on nature's earliest plan,
Were form'd to loath, and to be loath'd by man,
Which ow'd their birth to nastiness and spite,
Deadly to touch, and hateful to the sight,
Creatures, which, when admitted in the ark,
Their Saviour shun'd, and rankled in the dark,

Found place *within*; marking her noisome road
With poison's trail, here crawl'd the bloated Toad;
*There* webs were spread of more than common size,
And half-starved spiders prey'd on half-starv'd flies;
In quest of food, Efts strove in vain to crawl;
Slugs, pinch'd with hunger, smear'd the slimy wall;
The cave around with hissing serpents rung;
On the damp roof unhealthy vapour hung,
And FAMINE, *by her children always known,*
*As proud as poor, here* fix'd her native throne.

[ll. 319–34]

The dialogue between Jockey and Sawney (ll. 343–402) parodies
the opening scene of Ramsay's *Gentle Shepherd*,[25] so we know that
Churchill is maintaining his pose of the pastoral poet. The scene ends
as Famine rises from her throne to offer the disheartened swains a
promise of better times to come: although we are "nature's bastards"
(l. 425) and, like the Israelites, have wandered years in "a barren
desart" (l. 449), soon

we shall seize rich plains
Where milk with honey flows, and plenty reigns.
With some few natives join'd, some *pliant* few,
Who worship int'rest, and our track pursue,
There shall we, tho' the wretched people grieve,
Ravage at large, nor ask the owner's leave.

[ll. 449–54]

The figure of Famine serves to objectify after a fashion Churchill's
thought about the consequences of a growing Scottish influence in
English politics, diplomacy, and trade. In lines 455–86, particularly,
Famine *is* Churchill, or may as well be: failing to resemble him in
what she says only by the putative difference in their names. Twice
Famine refers to "traitors" in an impossible sense from the Scottish
point of view (ll. 510–17), and through her whole speech, moreover,
she represents her plan for overthrowing the English in so brutally
cynical a light (much in the fashion of Oldham's Loyola) that there is
no mistaking whose feelings inform her words; her plan is a "snare"

to catch the "fond" English (ll. 497–98), or an "engine of deceit" (l. 547).

The ironic pose of pastoral poet is silently dropped as soon as the dialogue between Jockey and Sawney ends. Rather than impersonating someone else, Churchill makes Famine impersonate himself, and her speech is not ironic: she says in so many words what Churchill means. That the ventriloquist's dummy should, in Churchill's case, turn out to sound just like the ventriloquist, is perhaps not surprising.

### The "Dedication to Warburton"

This short, unfinished piece has drawn some modern critical attention, notably from Yvor Winters, who finds in it "a number of feelings belonging neither to irony nor to eulogy, but capable of joining with both."[26] My own consideration of the poem is limited really to the one question of what happens to the ironic assumption with which it begins; for though it is an intriguing poem in other ways, Alan Fisher has already explored them well.[27]

While Churchill had attacked William Warburton before in *The Duellist* (ll. 667–810), he had been writing as a political partisan and as the friend of Wilkes. The attack, then, was obvious and direct: Warburton is "a false Saint, and true Hypocrite" (l. 810). The occasion of writing a dedication to his sermons, however, puts Churchill in the very different and surely somewhat unaccustomed role of clergyman.

"Health to great Gloster," he begins, playing the part of Warburton's eulogist. The role is of course ironic, and in that respect essentially different from the various roles in which he liked to appear in earlier poems: whether as critic of actors, of pastoral poetry, or as outraged moralist (e.g., *The Times*), he could appear fundamentally as himself. Here in the *Dedication*, though, it is necessary to begin with a kind of self-denial, and that on such a tempting occasion, as well.

Churchill gives lines 33–72 to the subject of Warburton, undertaking there to analyze his pretended admiration for the Bishop. The method is to reject as reasons for his admiration all the outward appearances of Warburton's rank and attainments:

> 'Tis not thy Name, though that indeed is great,
> 'Tis not the tinsel trumpery of state,
> 'Tis not thy Title, Doctor tho' thou art,
> 'Tis not thy Mitre, which hath won my heart.
>
> [ll. 33–36]

By minimizing these and other conventional emblems of Warburton's right to be praised—his physical appearance, birth, ancestry—Churchill succeeds in reducing it to a matter of the "inward Man" (l. 61), who deserves to be praised because he is a man of "virtue." Naturally this procedure throws into ironic relief the whole question of whether Warburton actually is virtuous.

Still keeping to the premise of a dedication, Churchill now begins to illustrate his "indebtedness" to Warburton as a mentor and an inspiring example. As a young man, Churchill says, I hoped to find in Warburton a guide who "might show me what is Taste, by what is not" (l. 104). But how could I think that this "virtuous" man,

> the servant of his Maker sworn,
> The servant of his Saviour, would be torn
> From their embrace, and leave that dear employ,
> The cure of souls, his duty and his joy,
> For toys like mine, and waste his precious time,
> On which so much depended, for a rime?
>
> [ll. 115–20]

Here the irony has become more transparent, since of course Warburton did in fact "waste his precious time" on the "rimes" of Pope and Shakespeare.

The indirect ridicule which Churchill so far has more or less managed to sustain collapses suddenly with this comment on Warburton's denunciation of Wilkes's *Essay on Woman*:

> O Glorious Man, thy zeal I must commend,
> Tho' it depriv'd me of my dearest friend.
> The real motives of thy anger known,
> WILKES must the justice of that anger own;
> And, could thy bosom have been bar'd to view,
> Pitied himself, in turn had pitied you.
>
> [ll. 145–50]

The more that Churchill allows himself to refer to his own true feelings, as in calling Wilkes his "dearest friend," the greater the strain on the ironic pretense. His commendation of Warburton's "zeal" becomes absurdly out of key when he adds that it "depriv'd me of my dearest friend." Praise finally turns into blame with "in turn had pitied you."

Before the poem breaks off, Churchill issues Warburton a warning. By now the eulogist has completely disappeared, leaving in his place the Churchill who despises the man he had so earnestly pretended to admire a moment ago. In this final passage Warburton is perched high (and precariously) atop the wheel of Fortune, and Churchill tells us that it is only "for want of smooth hypocrisy" that he must gaze up at him from below.

> Let GLOSTER well remember, how he rose,
> Nor turn his back on men who made him great;
> Let Him not, gorg'd with pow'r, and drunk with state,
> Forget what once he was, tho' now so high;
> How low, how mean, and full as poor as I.
>
> [ll. 176–80]

Here Churchill has returned to the Warburton of *The Duellist*— "gorg'd with pow'r, and drunk with state." The ironic dedication based on false values in Warburton ends as a serious warning that can only be justified by saying, in so many words, how false those values are.

It would seem that irony as a mode of satire demands more from Churchill than he is willing to give. It particularly requires him to give up the thing he wants most to express, which is his unpretending and "honest" self. Hence, irony as Churchill makes use of it—which is not very often—generally tends to resolve into some more directly expressive form.

The ironic satire that we associate especially with Pope, Swift, and the Scriblerus Club is not designed to reveal the personality of the satirist but instead to deal with a world that is envisioned as foolish and corrupt. Ironic expression also implies a kind of code communication with a knowing audience, and for that reason obviously does not lend itself to self-expression as the more direct method of invective does. In fact there is a certain sense in which Churchill's invective should be regarded as a theme rather than a method of his satire: he routinely connects the fact that he is writing invective with some feature of his character—his honesty, his rage—so that the author's choice of a method also seems a choice of personality. His invective in this sense is a method of self-portrayal as well as a method simply of ridiculing something. I am inclined to see this, for instance, in the fact that he became famous, and liked becoming famous, as "The Bruiser."[28]

## IRONY AND INVECTIVE: CHURCHILL TO BYRON

The satiric method of direct abuse as Churchill makes use of it may be said to be more obviously a means of expressing strong personal feeling—more obviously, because while any kind of invective is a display of strong personal feeling, in Churchill's case there is seldom any attempt to conceal this fact, to make the abusive language seem to attach itself to the abused rather than the abuser. Churchill himself plays such an important role in the satire he writes that one is inclined to regard the invective not so much as a quality or manner of the work as of the man.

In the years after his death he commonly figures as the type of the intemperate satirist, and in this respect he stands out all the more because of the disesteem in which such satire had been held from the early part of the century onwards. In the satire after Churchill there are certain instances in which the strength and style of attack is like his: frequently in Chatterton, only occasionally in Mason and Cowper, and more or less regularly in the ever-obscure, ever-unflagging tradition of political satire and party poems. On the whole, however, the Churchillian manner does not reappear as a sustained, conscious mode of literary satire until the days of Gifford at the end of the century.

Gifford, even more than Churchill, allows his invective to seem to be a part of his personality, and it is usual to find him indulging in a kind of wholesale namecalling which, by its lack of any patterning or indirection, forces the reader to think of it as proceeding in accordance with the emotional demands of the author rather than the artistic or formal demands of the work. Epithets like "idiotic," "trash," or "drivel" typify the effect (these from the *Baviad*). Or this, from the same poem:

> Let such, a task congenial to their powers,
> At sales and auctions waste their morning hours,
> While the dull noon away in Christie's fane,
> And snore the evening out at Drury lane;
> Lull'd by the twang of Bensley's nasal note,
> And the hoarse croak of Kemble's foggy throat.[29]

One reason that Gifford's invective in the *Baviad* and *Maeviad* so often produces an impression about the *author* is that the thing he is attacking, the Della Cruscan poetry, is hopelessly inconsequential, even by the measure of his own time, so that his ridicule is distressingly overbearing (a satiric situation that often applies in Churchill as well). Most of the contemporary reviews of the *Baviad* expressed agreement as to the worthlessness of the Della Cruscan movement, for example, but also reflected on the needless pitch of Gifford's indignation; the reviewers, in other words, generally considered the poem as an expression of the author's personality.[30] But Gifford, again like Churchill, invites such a response by his habit of interweaving the abuse of his object with allusions to himself, thus calling our attention to himself as the source of the abuse:

> And may not I—now this pernicious pest,
> This metromania, creeps thro' every breast;
> Now fools and children void their brains by loads,
> And itching grandams spawl lascivious odes;
> Now lords and dukes, curs'd with a sickly taste,
> While Burns' pure healthful nurture runs to waste,
> Lick up the spittle of the bed rid muse,
> And riot on the sweepings of the stews;
> Say, may not I expose . . .[31]

A similar effect, though a somewhat milder manner, is evident in T. J. Mathias (who thought highly of Gifford):

> Enough for me great Shakespeare's words to hear,
> Though but in common with the vulgar ear;
> Without one note, or horn-book in my head,
> Ritson's coarse trash, or lumber of the dead.[32]

And perhaps it is the early Byron who gives us the best illustration of this kind of satire, which consists not simply of invective but of invec-

tive clearly labeled as the expression of the writer's intemperate feeling. This is basically the post–Augustan "Juvenal," as in the opening
lines of *English Bards and Scotch Reviewers*:

> Still must I hear?—shall hoarse Fitzgerald bawl
> His creaking couplets in a tavern hall,
> And I not sing, lest, haply, Scotch reviews
> Should dub me scribbler, and denounce my muse?
> Prepare for rhyme—I'll publish, right or wrong:
> Fools are my theme, let satire be my song.
>
> [ll. 1–6]

The effect I have been describing is to be identified chiefly with the
"Juvenalian" satire at the end of the century, and while it is consistent
with the overall emphasis in post–Augustan satire upon the work as an
emotional extension of the writer, it is an exception to the rule in that
the kind of emotion involved is the violent hostility that invective implies. As a rule, in fact, the satire after Churchill is typically much less
abusive, though at the same time no less direct in expressing the satirist's true feelings.

Anstey, for one, may be taken as an illustration of this more nearly
normative mode. Here is Simkin Blunderhead's account of Widow
Quicklackit, from Letter 11 of the *New Bath Guide*:

> But who is that bombazine lady so gay,
> So profuse of her beauties in sable array?
> How she rests on her heel, how she turns out her toe,
> How she pulls down her stays, with her head up, to shew
> Her lily-white bosom that rivals the snow!
> 'Tis the widow Quicklackit, whose husband last week,
> Poor Stephen, went suddenly forth in a pique,
> And push'd off his boat for the *Stygian* creek:
> Poor Stephen! he never return'd from the bourn,
> But left the disconsolate widow to mourn:
> Three times did she faint when she heard of the news;
> Six days did she weep, and all comfort refuse;
> But Stephen, no sorrow, no tears can recall:
> So she hallows the seventh, and comes to the ball.[33]

The method is ironic, certainly, in that Anstey's satirical attitude is expressed only indirectly, through Simkin's ingenuous point of view. But neither is there any mistaking Anstey's point of view. The familiarity of the type he is satirizing, the obviousness of her behavior at the ball, the cheerfulness of the allusions to her husband's demise—all combine to make the irony as transparent as if we were hearing the lines read aloud with a sarcastic intonation. Moreover, the tone of tolerant amusement in these lines belongs really to Anstey rather than Simkin: that is to say, the tone is Anstey's usual one, and in that respect he is not particularly dissembling his own satirical feelings for the sake of impersonating the character of Simkin, and as in the case of Churchill and Famine, Simkin in effect impersonates Anstey.

In the Epilogue to the *New Bath Guide*, in the "Appendix" to *The Patriot*, and elsewhere when Anstey introduces himself directly as the author, his tone is virtually always the same: ironically deprecating, whether directed at himself or at something or someone else. This tone becomes especially Anstey's own, independently of its belonging to a particular poem of his. So also in the case of William Mason, whose first satire (the *Heroic Epistle to Sir William Chambers*) is based on a technique of mocking Chambers' ideas by extending them ridiculously; it is very stylishly brought off, especially in the consistency of the mock-serious treatment—what the *Monthly Review* noted as a "vein of fine solemn irony." [34] In his other satires, however, Mason abandons this consistency in favor of a more direct representation of his point of view, and instead of a mock-serious work, like the *Heroic Epistle*, we have a mock-serious voice within the work, as in this from *An Epistle to Dr. Shebbeare*:

> Come, then, Shebbeare! and hear thy bard deliver
> Unpaid-for praises to thy pension-giver.
> Hear me, like T..k.r, swear, "so help me, muse!
> I write not for preferment's golden views."
> But hold—'tis on thy province to intrude:
> I would be loyal, but would not be rude.
> To thee, my veteran, I his fame consign;
> Take thou St. James's, be St. Stephen's mine. [35]

Mason is ridiculing Dr. Shebbeare as a self-serving panegyricist, and he does this in words that must be taken ironically; so to that extent the mode of the satire is irony or a "speaking by contraries." But Mason in this passage also reminds us constantly that *he* is saying what is being said, and as a result the mode of the satire is also the manner of the satirist.

The mode of Peter Pindar's satire is almost always that of burlesque inflation: a ridiculously misplaced "enlargement" of the satiric object, usually accompanied by broad expressions of humility, reverential awe, sincerity, or whatever the appropriate (pretended) emotion on Peter's part. Such inflation, as in the case of Mason, is technically a type of irony, in that Peter frequently says what he does not in fact mean, but says it always with a view to sounding as if he doesn't mean it. To take one example from his *Poetical and Congratulatory Epistle to James Boswell, Esq. on His Journal of a Tour to the Hebrides with the Celebrated Dr. Johnson* (1786), consider the degree to which his mocking tone calls attention to itself in these lines on Boswell-as-historian:

> I see thee stuffing, with a hand uncouth,
> An old dried Whiting in thy Johnson's mouth;
> And lo! I see, with all his might and main,
> Thy Johnson spit the Whiting out again.
> Rare Anecdotes! 'tis Anecdotes like these
> That bring thee glory, and the Million please:
> On these shall future times delighted stare,
> Thou charming Haberdasher of Small Ware.
> Stewart and Robertson from thee shall learn,
> The *simple* charms of History to discern:
> To thee, fair History's palm shall Livy yield,
> And Tacitus to Bozzy leave the field . . .[36]

The ostentatiously mocking manner is at the heart of Peter's satire and may be described as an attempt to achieve the effect, in written form, of spoken sarcasm or of theatrical mock-seriousness.

Another example shows Peter at his characteristic best, for which reason I am quoting more than is strictly necessary to illustrate the point. The title is *The Rights of Kings, or Loyal Odes to Disloyal*

*Academicians* (1791), and Peter's note "To the Reader" will serve to explain the occasion:

> The foundation of the following Odes is simply this: The President of the Royal Academy, happy to be able to gratify our amiable Monarch in the minutest of his predilections, reported lately to the Academicians his Majesty's desire, that a Mr. Laurence might be added to the list of R.A.s; his Majesty, from his *superior knowledge* in Painting, being *perfectly convinced* of this young Artist's *uncommon* abilities, and consequently fair pretensions to the honour. Notwithstanding the Royal *wish*, and the *wish* of the President, and (under the rose!!!) the *wish* of Mr. Benjamin West, the Windsor Oracle of Paint, and Painter of History, the R.A.s received the annunciation of his Majesty's *wish*, Sir Joshua's *wish*, Mr. West's *wish*, with the most ineffable *sang froid*; not to call it by the harder name, *disgust*. The annunciation happening on the night of an election of Associates, at which Mr. Laurence ought to have been elected an Associate (a step necessary to the more exalted one of R.A.), behold the obstinacy of these *royal* Mules!—the number of votes in favour of Mr. Laurence amounted to just *three*; and that of his Opponent, Mr. Wheatley, to *sixteen*!!! Indignant and loyal Reader! the Lyric Muse, who has uniformly attacked *meanness, folly, impudence, avarice,* and *ignorance*, from her cradle, caught fire at the above important event; and most loyally poured forth the following Odes, replete with her *usual* sublimities.[37]

This note itself, albeit in prose, exemplifies the effect. One notices particularly the use of emphasis and punctuation to suggest the manner of a speaking voice. The first ode begins:

> Am I awake, or dreaming, O ye Gods?
> Alas! in *waking's* favour lie the odds.
>     The devil it is! Ah me, 'tis really so!
> How, Sirs? on Majesty's proud corns to tread!
> Messieurs Academicians, when you're *dead,*
>     *Where* can your Impudence hope to go?
>
> Refuse a Monarch's mighty orders!—
> It smells of Treason; on Rebellion borders.—
> Sdeath, Sirs! it was the Queen's fond wish as well,

That Master Laurence should come in.
Against a Queen so *gentle* to rebel!
This is another crying sin.

What! not oblige, in such a trifling thing,
So *sweet* a Queen, and such a *goodly* King? [38]

This is irony, certainly, but irony so highly visible as to make its effect
felt less as a realization of meaning—which is never doubtful—than
as a continued awareness of the speaker's presence and manner, the way
he "sounds." Peter himself is clearly concerned with the fact that the
method of his satire, the particular technique by which he expresses
his meaning, is also (and perhaps more importantly) to be identified
as an expression of his personality. Ode 3 of the *Lyric Odes to the Royal
Academicians* (1785), for instance, begins with Peter announcing a
change in satiric method, one which he represents simultaneously as
a change in personality:

One minute, gentle Irony, retire:
    Behold! I'm graver than a mustard-pot;
The Muse, with bile as hot as fire,
    Could call *fool, puppy, blockhead,* and what not? [39]

We find the same high degree of "visibility" in the various modes
of Byron's later poems, where irony clearly plays a role that is thematic
as well as merely technical or formal—a role, that is, as an essential
part of the personality Byron projects. In the following stanza from
*Beppo*, for example, the negligently sarcastic manner works not only
as a means of ridicule but also as a way of hitting off a certain "character" of Byron:

One hates an author that's *all author*, fellows
    In foolscap uniforms turn'd up with ink,
So very anxious, clever, fine, and jealous,
    One don't know what to say to them, or think,
Unless to puff them with a pair of bellows;
    Of coxcombry's worst coxcombs e'en the pink
Are preferable to these shreds of paper,
These unquench'd snuffings of the midnight taper.

[st. 75]

This of course is Byron the patrician amateur speaking, and in a style that very closely resembles that of his letters: "One hates an author that's *all author* ..."

The ironical manner in Byron, particularly in *Don Juan* and the *Vision of Judgment*, adds a thematic dimension to his verse, in the skepticism and self-doubt it characteristically evokes, as in this passage from the *Vision of Judgment*:

> 'God save the king!' It is a large economy
>     In God to save the like; but if he will
> Be saving, all the better; for not one am I
>     Of those who think damnation better still:
> I hardly know too if not quite alone am I
>     In this small hope of better future ill
> By circumscribing, with some slight restriction,
> The eternity of hell's hot jurisdiction.
>
> I know this is unpopular; I know
>     'Tis blasphemous; I know one may be damn'd
> For hoping no one else may e'er be so;
>     I know my catechism; I know we are cramm'd
> With the best doctrines till we quite o'erflow;
>     I know that all save England's church have shamm'd,
> And that the other twice two hundred churches
> And synagogues have made a *damn'd* bad purchase.
>
> God help us all! God help me too! I am,
>     God knows, as helpless as the devil can wish,
> And not a whit more difficult to damn
>     Than is to bring to land a late-hook'd fish,
> Or to the butcher to purvey the lamb;
>     Not that I'm fit for such a noble dish
> As one day will be that immortal fry
> Of almost everybody born to die.
>
> [st. 13–15]

This is not the only effect Byron seeks in his use of irony, as he is, for example, equally fond of enhancing his narratives with the comic irony of understatement after the manner of Fielding. What the illustration from the *Vision of Judgment* serves to typify, I think, is the double effect of his mock-seriousness, which culminates one moment in a satiric point ("I know that all save England's church have shamm'd"), and another moment in self-display ("God help me too!").

The term "romantic irony," with which it is to some degree proper to associate Byron, implies an emphasis on viewpoint rather than technique, and rather refers to a characteristic attitude or personality, a certain sort of man, than to the mode of expression of a literary work. There is no corresponding term "Augustan irony," of course, but that may very well be because the irony of that period has no identifying philosophical character. The same thing applies, less obviously, to the difference between Augustan and post-Augustan forms of invective, since in the latter case, especially the self-assertive "Juvenalian" invective, technique acquires meaning in itself; and the weapon, in short, defines the user.

Thus, while the method of ridicule in later eighteenth-century satire is sometimes direct and sometimes not, and while some of this satire consists of severe invective and some of ironic falsification of literal meaning, almost all of it shows in common a tendency for the mode of the satire to appear more directly and definitely as the manner of speaking of the satirist. When we speak of the mode of the satire in a piece by Peter Pindar or William Gifford, to take two of the most consistent examples, we think mainly of the manner in which the satirist presents himself as speaking, rather than the manner in which the work presents itself.

Indeed in the satire of this period the purely formal aspect of the work plays a considerably less important role in determining how the work is to be taken than was the case in the Restoration and early eighteenth century. This change would accord with the general relaxation of the generic concept of literature, as a result of which it is to be expected that the satirist would not seek to have his meaning understood in terms of mock-genres such as the parody litany, mock-encomium, and mock-heroic. Or if he does attempt this kind of satire, as Richard Owen Cambridge does in the *Scribleriad*, and Churchill in the *Dedication to Warburton*, the writer seems unable to withdraw completely and let the work speak for itself. Cambridge, unlike Churchill, does not admit any inconsistency within the text itself; yet in the preface to the poem still feels it is necessary to explain, at considerable length, the point that he has tried to write a "pure" mock-heroic, and that his readers should understand that the things he says in it are always to be taken ironically. Such earnest overexplanation is difficult to imagine in Pope, and surely is related to the difference between what Pope expects of his audience and what Cambridge expects of his.

## CHAPTER 6

# Author and Audience

IN THE *Tale of a Tub*, Swift's Grub-street Hack advertises a list of his forthcoming productions, two of which are *A Panegyric upon the World* and *A Modest Defence of the Proceedings of the Rabble in all Ages*. These imaginary works exemplify the pandering contract into which the Hack has entered with his audience or "the world," a relationship between them which Swift sees as vicious due to the mindlessly admiring attitude it requires of the writer. Its ridiculousness lies in the Hack's acceptance of the world or the proceedings of the rabble merely because they are what they are and not because they are witty or dull, good or evil.

The other extreme could be illustrated by Swift's professed aim of writing to vex the world rather than divert it. Satire, not panegyric, is then the normal response of a sane man to the world. One proof of this is history, which to Swift and many Augustans is a species of involuntary satire. For "such are most human Actions," writes Edward Young, "that to relate, is to expose them."[1]

Both attitudes toward the world, the one that Swift parodies and the one he takes seriously, may be used as reference points in considering the satirist's relationship with his audience. When I speak of the author–audience relationship, I mean the relationship as it is represented within the work, explicitly or implicitly. In that sense it is one of the conventions of a literary work, and more particularly, constitutes the author's idealized view of his audience and of his role with respect to them. Here also a distinction should be made between the author's conventionalized relationship with his audience, those whom he pretends to be addressing, and his (also conventionalized) attitude toward the world. The Augustan Tory satirists, for instance, take a hostile or "gloomy" attitude toward the world and typically appear to be addressing themselves to an exclusive minority, an audience distinguished by its not being representative of the world. So this distinction between their audience and the world in general is insisted upon and exploited by these satirists.

On the other hand, naturally enough, the less disaffected the author's view of the world, the more representative of it his putative audience may be made to seem. To take one such instance from early eighteenth-century literature: Steele invites us to think that the female readers he pretends to address in the *Tatler* form a typical part of the world, at least as the world is envisioned in the *Tatler* (which needless to say is not the way it is envisioned in Pope's work). In this case the distinction collapses, such that "audience" and "World" can be thought of interchangeably.

The conventionalized author–audience relationship doesn't necessarily resemble the real historical relationship between author and audience. Pope's represented audience is much smaller than his real one actually was. But of course it may also happen that the convention will correspond to reality, as with Mr. Spectator, who affects to take the Town for his audience and is in turn taken by the Town and read as widely as he pretends to be.

Eighteenth-century poetry characteristically seeks the form of a conversation or an epistle.[2] In this connection one thinks naturally of Pope, whose use of dialogue or epistolary conventions may be taken as an indication that he views poetry (ideally) as a form of communication. This representation of poetry also acquires a special importance for Pope and, to a lesser extent, other Augustan satirists, in that it suits the expression of an elitist view. Thus Pope addresses himself to certain people only—to Bolingbroke or Swift or Arbuthnot—to the seeming exclusion of the larger and more vulgar audience of "the world."

This is the divided-audience motif that Watt identifies as characteristic of Augustan satire, or at least of Augustan Tory satire (discussed above, chap. 5). In the case of the good-natured satire that Addison and Steele advocate and practice in the *Tatler* and *Spectator*, however, the relationship between author and audience takes a different form altogether, one closer to that which Swift caricatures in the Grub-street Hack. The satire in these periodicals, such as it is, obviously is not what we think of when using the term "Augustan satire." And while it would be improper to attempt to relate Addison and Steele too significantly to the tradition of Augustan verse satire, I do think they serve as an illustration within the same period of another version of the author–audience relationship—one which incidentally comes to be the dominant version in the literature of the later eighteenth century.

"Good-natured satire" turns out to be an elusive model, more often encountered during the period as an example of what real satire is not than of what it is. Theoretically it is possible to qualify as a satirist and also as a good-natured man, but practically speaking it seldom happens. The two terms "good nature" and "satire," in other words, are sufficiently incompatible as to force in practice a choice between them. Good nature, in fact, joins much more successfully with comedy than with satire, and when Steele and Addison talk about good-natured satire, they seem to mean something that would be more aptly called comedy, in the sense of a tolerant amusement. Sir Roger de Coverley, for instance, is in one sense an object of ridicule in the *Spectator* papers; yet in later literature, especially in the novel, he emerges as an important model for a type of comic (not satiric) characterization.

Compared to the major figures of ridicule in Augustan verse satire —Achitophel, Sporus—Sir Roger reflects a much more tolerant moral view of the world on the part of his creators. Like the Ned Softlys and other such objects of satire in the *Spectator*, he might even be regarded as a member of the audience for whom the papers are being written— in the sense that he is not morally rejected but rather shown to be a part, and perhaps even an essential part, of the social scene. Certainly there is the implication throughout the *Tatler* and *Spectator* that the writers find the type-characters they satirize from among the audience of their readers.

The starting point of the *Tatler* and *Spectator* is a certain acceptance of contemporary society on its own terms. "Wherever I see a Cluster of People," Mr. Spectator says, "I always mix with them, though I never open my lips but in my own Club."[3] Mr. Spectator develops a relationship with his audience which is not "vexed" but conciliatory and reassuring; far from excluding part of the world as his audience, he strives to broaden the base of literature by addressing himself to the town as a whole. When he represents himself as passing invisibly among the citizens, or when he publishes their "letters" to him, he insinuates in effect that he is one of their own kind—more knowing, more refined perhaps, and certainly their teacher, but one of them all the same.

Likewise, the satire in the *Tatler* and *Spectator* papers shows an awareness of this wider, more general audience. We will remember that Steele in discussing the various aspects of "false" satire says that ". . . when the sentence [of reproof] appears to arise from personal hatred or passion, it is not then made the cause of mankind but a misunderstanding between two persons. . . . You must make your satire the concern of society in general if you would have it regarded."[4] At the bottom of such a statement lies a practical interest in appealing to the audience of society in general, much the same consideration as that which later prompted Fielding to give up his ironical method of writing in the *Jacobite's Journal* (see above, chap. 5).

Addison and Steele also are genuinely interested in reforming the manners and taste of their audience, and if we can believe what Gay said about their practical success at this program in his famous remarks in *The Present State of Wit*, then their claims as to the social value of satire must be taken as more than merely rhetorical. Theoretically at least, the "happy ending" of satire is reform. It is something that takes place, or is supposed to take place, outside the work itself. In comedy, as opposed to satire, a change for the better, a happy ending, is represented as taking place within the work. But whether this happy ending is a formal part of the work or is presumed to be a social extension of it, as with the satire in the *Spectator*, it implies a more or less tolerant view of society or "the world." In the very broad terms of myth analysis, for instance, the happy ending of comedy is generally thought of as the integration of society, the harmonious assimilation of disruptive antisocial forces.

But in cases where the satirist's moral view of the world is extremely intolerant, as in the later Pope and Swift, there is of course no such suggestion, no pretense even that any reform will take place as a consequence of the satire. The *Spectator* had come to its own happy ending in which manners were at last reformed. But Pope has universal darkness bury all; and Swift in the *Verses on the Death of Dr. Swift* sees the ascendancy of the Whigs as a synecdoche of national ruin. Pope's insistence on the hopeless inefficacy of satire allows him to push the logic of his rhetorical situation to the point where he must (figuratively) give it all up, as he tells us in his note on the last line of the *Epilogue to the Satires*:

> This was the last poem of the kind printed by our author, with a resolution to publish no more; but to enter thus, in the most plain and solemn manner he could, a sort of PROTEST against that insuperable corruption and depravity of manners, which he had been so unhappy as to live to see. Could he have hoped to have amended any, he had continued those attacks; but bad men were grown so shameless and so powerful, that Ridicule was become as unsafe as it was ineffectual. The Poem raised him, as he knew it would, some enemies; but he had reasons to be satisfied with the approbation of good men, and the testimony of his own conscience.

Here Pope makes the widest possible division between those he is addressing and seeking to please, the "good men" or even simply his own conscience, and those he is satirizing and would, in other circumstances, try to reform. Having resolved to "publish no more," he has in a manner of speaking no more audience at all—except in the sense that he is his own audience, responding to himself with the testimony of his own conscience.

Post–Augustan satirists, like Pope and Swift, almost always speak of "the world" with a certain contempt. But while Pope and Swift appear earnest and sometimes passionate in their hostility to the world, the tone in post–Augustan satire is characteristically more cynical, resigned, matter-of-fact, or amused and skeptical. Pope and Swift seem to be saying that the world is moving in an unacceptable direction. It is a major point with them, and they embody it in their satire as a horror-struck vision of what the world is coming to: the arithmetical, amoral logic of the *Modest Proposal*, the "sunken" esthetics of *Peri Bathous*. For Churchill or Peter Pindar or the *Anti–Jacobin* writers, however, society in general simply seems unacceptable to begin with, and the main point usually involves how the individual is supposed to respond, given the fact that he finds the world unanswerable to himself. Burns, as it happens, builds an entire poem around this idea, in the form of advice to a young friend:

> Ye'll try the world my lad;
> And ANDREW dear believe me,
> Ye'll find mankind an unco squad,
> And muckle they may grieve ye . . .

We are out of the realm of satire here, for the poet's object lies not in making the point that mankind is "an unco squad" but in telling Andrew how to deal with mankind:

> To catch dame Fortune's golden smile,
> Assiduous wait upon her;
> And gather gear by ev'ry wile
> That's justified by Honour:
> Not for to *hide* it in a *hedge*,
> Nor for a *train-attendant*;
> But for the glorious priviledge
> Of being *independant*.[5]

The strong sense of a divided audience typical in Augustan satire largely disappears in later eighteenth-century satirical poetry. Specifically, it is no longer usual to find the satirist addressing his satire to one of his fellow-members of a righteous minority. The practice is not abandoned, of course: several of the satiric epistles arising out of the Churchill–Colman–Thornton–Lloyd coterie fall into this category— they being successors after a fashion to the Scriblerus Club; and Gifford and Mathias both make use of the author–friend dialogue convention. More often, though, the satire is addressed to no one in particular, such that we may have the personal speaking tone of a conversation or an epistle without its actually being represented as that.

This is the case in many of Churchill's poems, including *The Ghost*,

*The Prophecy of Famine, Gotham.* It is also true of Cowper, whose moral–satiric verse essays, unlike Pope's, are not formally addressed to a particular listener or audience. Indeed the model Cowper most often seems to have in mind is that of the sermon rather than the epistle or dialogue. Instead of a divided audience—the morally select group (the Bathursts and Arbuthnots) to whom the writer addresses himself, and the general audience of mankind who are the objects of his moralizing and satire—Cowper addresses himself directly to mankind, exhorting or criticizing or warning them in the style of a preacher to his congregation:

> Take, if ye can, ye careless and supine,
> Counsel and caution from a voice like mine!
> Truths, that the theorist could never reach,
> And observation taught me, I would teach.[6]

*Table Talk* (1782) uses the device of the interlocutor, but Cowper's other satires do not; instead, he has a distinctive habit of anticipating responses as from someone in his audience: in *Truth* (1782), following the well-known passage in which he compares the two types of servants, the ingratiating but faithless Tom, and the loyal Charles, Cowper writes:

> Now which stands highest in your serious thought?
> Charles, without doubt, say you—and so he ought;
> One act, that from a thankful heart proceeds,
> Excels ten thousand mercenary deeds.
>
> [ll. 221–24]

Here the relations between author and audience are very close, almost collaborative. Yet the "you" of these lines is not identified as someone (a friend, for instance) with whom the author is communicating exclusively. On the contrary, the implication is that he is simply the reader.

Not only does Cowper not divide his audience or make exclusivist distinctions within it, he strives for the effect of including all social and moral categories in his addresses. Often he will open up on a new topic by addressing himself to the special group he intends to speak to: "Artist, attend!" (*Truth*, l. 171), or

To you, then, tenants of life's middle state,
Securely plac'd between the small and great,
Whose character, yet undebauch'd, retains
Two thirds of all the virtue that remains,
Who, wise yourselves, desire your sons should learn
Your wisdom and your ways—to you I turn.
Look round you on a world perversely blind . . .[7]

Cowper shows always an earnest desire to communicate with his audience, to instruct and improve them. His audience *is* the world (hence his characteristic of addressing first one category of people, then another, and so on); and he is much more optimistic than the later Pope, than Churchill, Lloyd, Peter Pindar, Gifford, or Byron, about the possibility of actually reforming the world, chiefly because he, unlike them, sets out upon the asumption that expostulating with the world will do more real good than satirizing it.

We can see in Cowper a willingness to address himself to anyone in his audience, without distinction, even to those members of the audience who in a strictly satiric context would be classified as enemies, that is, the people the author wants to reform. The technique of addressing a satire to the very man (or men) being satirized scarcely ever occurs in Augustan satire, where the normal practice is to address the satire (if it is to be addressed to anybody) to a friend. Or if the enemy is addressed, it is by way of one of the ironic forms such as the mock-panegyric.[8]

The story is different with the post–Augustan satirists, who frequently write satires in the form of epistles or addresses directly to the satiric victim himself. In fact, this is probably the one most complete turnabout that takes place during the century in the management of author–audience conventions. There are dozens of examples: Churchill's *Epistle to William Hogarth*, Mason's *Epistle to Dr. Shebbeare*, any number of Peter Pindar's poems "to" so-and-so, Burns's *Address to the Unco Guid*, the Dedication verses to Southey at the beginning of *Don Juan*. By and large the manner is direct (if abusive) and represents the author's true feelings realistically. In some instances one gets the impression of reading an actual letter in verse rather than verses in the form of a letter. Burns's *Reply to a Trimming Epistle*

*Received from a Tailor* (1786) begins, "What ails ye now, ye lousie bitch, / To thresh my back at sic a pitch?" It is amusing to wonder what Steele, in light of his concern for keeping the satire from sounding like a personal quarrel, would have made of Burns.

As for the addressees of these hostile epistles, besides individuals like Hogarth or Southey, and abstract groups who have something in common morally, like Cowper's "ye careless and supine," occupational groups are a favorite choice: Peter Pindar's long-suffering Royal Academicians, for instance, or, particularly, the Critics. Churchill's *Apology*, for example, is addressed "To the Critical Reviewers." So is one of Peter Pindar's earliest pieces, of which the title should give a sufficient hint: *A Poetical, Supplicating, Modest, and Affecting Epistle to Those Literary Colossuses, the Reviewers* (1778).

These are partly satires on critics—one of the commonest kinds of satire in the period—but they are also, to some extent, public replies to the critics (or in Peter Pindar's unusual case, a plea for praise in advance of his publishing something). John Hall-Stevenson's wretched *Two Lyric Epistles: or, Margery the Cook Maid to the Critical Review* (1762), for instance, is specifically a reply to what the *Critical Review* had said about his *Fables for Grown Gentlemen* (1761), even to the extent of including some footnote references to particular statements in the original review article.[9]

In view of the Augustan satirist's habit of disdaining "the mob" and pretending at least to restrict his addresses to the few who like himself are above the many, it is interesting, as a footnote on the democratization of satire, to find Cowper writing *An Address to the Mob on Occasion of the Late Riot at the House of Sir Hugh Palliser* (written 1778, published 1890). In it he is certainly scornful enough of the mob:

> And is it thus, ye base and blind,
> And fickle as the shifting wind,
> Ye treat a warrior staunch and true,
> Grown old in combating for you?

The principle of aristocracy does not seem in much danger here, but of course that is not the point. Cowper is rebuking the mob in order to shame them, the very non–Augustan implication being that the mob is capable of shame, and of being communicated with.

More intriguing still is an anonymous political satire entitled *A Dialogue . . . between a Noble Lord and the Mob* and printed in the *New Foundling Hospital for Wit*. This poem treats one of the London riots—this one the so-called Merchants' Address riot—that took place in early 1769, amid the popular turmoil over John Wilkes's disputed election to Parliament. All the writer's sympathy is with the mob. The ineffectual nobleman (possibly Lord Talbot) who has been commissioned to disperse them concludes his plea by saying that the King "would lay down his life for the people's protection," and the mob are made to reply,

> Oh! God bless the k———, he's the best of mankind;
> We wish those about him were all of his mind;
> No guards would be wanting to keep us in awe,
> As we honour his name, and we reverence the law.
> Let elections be free; and whoever we chuse,
> His seat in the house you should never refuse:
> And if great men were honest, the poor would be quiet;
> So yourselves you may thank for this bustle and riot.[10]

In the mind of one satirist, at least, the idea of the mob has come a long way.

In fact "the mob" is, in one sense, "the public." The more realistic style of address in satiric epistles, the new trick of addressing one's antagonist directly, the lessening of conventional restrictions upon the satirist to appear to be conversing or communicating only with a special audience, all point to a basic change in the way the relationship between author and audience is conceived and represented.

The entire post–Augustan period shows a gradual abandonment of epistolary and dialogue verse-conventions. That is, poetry is not so frequently represented as a definite act of communication between one person and another. Accordingly we have fewer reminders within the poem of who the writer's audience is. Such reminders as there are usually identify the audience as "the public" or, depending on the emphasis that is being sought, "the reader."

Churchill repeatedly tells us (partly as a political point) that it is only the public interest he cares about. Any debts he has he owes to "a gen'rous Public," who (this a literary point)

> made me what I Am.
> All that I have, They gave; just Mem'ry bears
> The grateful stamp, and what I am is Theirs.[11]

Churchill willingly portrays himself as a creature of the public, the main distinction for him being the one between those who are attached to the public interest, hence independent, and those who are the slaves of a private interest, such as patronage. It was the system of patronage that underlay the economics of writing at the beginning of the century and provided the context in which so many panegyrics and satires were written and in which the literary convention of the elite and the mob, the divided audience, must certainly be seen as having its roots. For "mob" and "elite," Churchill—along with Paul Whitehead, Chatterton, Mason, Peter Pindar, and most of the satirists of the period—substitutes another pair of terms, namely "slave" and "free man."

This substitution naturally implies a different economic basis for the writer, a change of employers of the sort described in Goldsmith's famous remark in 1760:

> At present, the few poets of England no longer depend on the Great for subsistence; they have now no other patrons but the public, and the public collectively considered, is a good and generous master.[12]

It also implies, rather obviously, a change in the writer's politics in the direction of "Wilkes and liberty." Burns is not the only satirist to identify with the democratic many rather than the aristocratic few: Peter Pindar calls himself the "Poet of the People," and elsewhere refers to "my good old friend, the Public."[13]

In the Epilogue appended to the second edition of the *New Bath Guide*, the conversation between the Guide (i.e., Anstey) and the "three Ladies of Piety, Learning, and Discretion" dramatizes clearly this newer conception of the relations between author and readers. These are essentially the same readers Steele was writing for, and while their taste and demands on the author are made to seem mildly ridiculous, underlying it all is the author's recognition that he must after all deal with them, that he cannot simply dismiss them. He doesn't especially like it, but he cannot do much about it either, except to complain and mutter. When one of the ladies starts to paste shut an offensive leaf in the book, the "book" calls out,

> Away with your paste! 'tis exceedingly hard
> Thus to torture and cramp an unfortunate bard:
> How my Muse will be shock'd, when she's just taking flight,
> To find that her pinions are fasten'd so tight!

And when the three ladies tell the Guide he would be better off writing novels, and proceed to give him an inane-sounding "receipt" for writing one, compounded of fake piety and sensationalism, he can only answer with "Damnation—(*aside.*) Well, ladies, I'll do what I can, / And ye'll bind it, I hope, with your *Duty of Man.*"[14] And thus he wanders off, muttering to himself. He has managed to glance ironically at their vulgar hypocrisy, of course, but he is more or less stuck with them.

A few further illustrations of the point. William Mason's first satire takes the form of an ironic address to the man being satirized, while his second satire, the *Heroic Postscript to the Public*, is a straightforward address to the readers of the first, "occasioned," as the subtitle has it, "by Their Favourable Reception of a Late Heroic Epistle to Sir William Chambers." In it Mason gratefully and sincerely acknowledges them as, in effect, his "good and generous master."

The author–public or author–reader form of the author–audience relationship seems to have been institutionalized first in the periodical essay and the novel, and only somewhat later in poetry. This pattern would make sense in view of the fact that for the essay and novel no other form of the relationship is really conceivable, since in the eighteenth century both of these genres are virtually brought into their existence by a widening public literacy. But by the end of the century even the poets are generally addressing themselves to the public, or more accurately, to "the reader."

Byron, for instance, adopts a "dear reader" manner from time to time in *Don Juan*. Unquestionably it owes something to the comic styles of address that had been worked out in the novel (specifically, in Fielding and Sterne): "I can't oblige you, reader, to read on; / That's your affair, not mine . . ." (canto 12, st. 87). Crabbe, though never in the habit of directly addressing his reader, occasionally alludes to his characters using the first person possessive pronoun, as "our Curate," "our poet," "our hero." Again it is a mainly novelistic trick of style, and has that odd effect of seeming to join the writer's and the reader's point of view. And even T. J. Mathias, whose *Pursuits of Literature* is cast in dialogue form, is found speaking to "the reader," directing his attention to this or that, in the vast editorial apparatus surrounding the poem proper.

We are used to hearing the seventeenth- or early eighteenth-century poet commending his poem to the protection of Lord Such-and-Such. The change that takes place later in the century may be characterized by a passage from an essay by John Hookham Frere which appeared in *The Microcosm* for 27 November 1786. He is concluding the essay with a poem—his own—and he says,

> I would wish to present to the perusal of my readers the following lines, not entirely foreign from some part of this essay; and at the same time admonish them that the smile of Melpomene at the birth of a poet is useless, without that of his readers on his publication.[15]

To return now to the distinction originally observed at the beginning of this chapter, that between "the world" and "the audience," one important problem remains to be considered. That is the seeming paradox in the two facts, already noted, that (1) post–Augustan satire shows a lack of interest in "the world" except as a background against which the satirist may display himself, a movement from a "public" to a more nearly "private" point of view, and that (2) this satire is also generally addressed "to the public." How is it that Byron can, in the space of fourteen lines at the end of *English Bards and Scotch Reviewers*, scorn the opinions of the world and also commend his poem to the world's good judgment?

> But now, so callous grown, so changed since youth,
> I've learned to think, and sternly speak the truth;

Learn'd to deride the critic's starch decree,
And break him on the wheel he meant for me;
To spurn the rod a scribbler bids me kiss,
*Nor care if courts and crowds applaud or hiss*:
Nay more, though all my rival rhymesters frown,
I too can hunt a poetaster down;
And, arm'd in proof, the gauntlet cast at once
To Scotch marauder, and to southern dunce.
Thus much I've dared; if my incondite lay
Hath wrong'd these righteous times, let others say:
*This, let the world, which knows not how to spare,*
*Yet rarely blames unjustly, now declare.*

[Italics mine]

The answer, I think, lies in the distinction that can be made between "the public," considered collectively as those who buy and read and talk about an author's book, and "the reader," considered individually as the person who is at any given moment "hearing" what the author is saying. A writer may address himself to the public, but only figuratively; since obviously the public is an abstraction and cannot read or write or be talked with. The act of reading and responding to what someone has written is private, of course, and though the author may be apt to think of the reader as part of "the public," the individual reader himself is not likely to. Hence the author, recognizing this, pretends to address the reader individually: it is usually "dear reader," not "dear readers."

When Byron makes a ringing claim on his own individuality, then, caring not if courts and crowds applaud or hiss, he is saying something that the reader may very well like to hear (and did in fact like to hear, if the history of poetry in the nineteenth century is a measure). Obviously the reader, not considering himself among the courts and crowds Byron disdains, will not feel himself to have been rejected or somehow left out, but instead will possibly regard Byron's attitude as like his own. So is it possible for multitudes of people to read sympathetically about Childe Harold setting his face against the multitudes. There may not be much difference after all between a poem in which Pope is shown talking to Arbuthnot about his feeling of moral isolation, and a poem in which Churchill or Byron simply expresses a feeling of moral isolation: except that different conventions do usually imply different views. In his feeling of moral isolation Pope seems to me very close to Churchill and Byron; but for Pope such private feelings, if they are to be expressed freely and directly in a poem, must be represented as feelings communicated to an understanding audience (however small) and not merely expressed without reference to what lies beyond the speaker.

## CHAPTER 7

# Satire and Poetry in Post-Augustan England

IT IS A FACT—one that I think will be acknowledged—that satire has not had any very important place in twentieth-century poetry. One has the fact brought home, for instance, in glancing over anthologies of verse satire, where such modern examples of the form as may be included might possibly demonstrate that verse satire is in fact still written, but little else; in no case could they tell anyone much about what modern poetry is like. Of course there are examples: one thinks of Auden, perhaps, or (casting about now) of Roy Campbell. But the feeling remains that the generic category "verse satire" is something out of keeping with the whole conception and practice of poetry in this century.

Why? One reason would be simply that we no longer think particularly in terms of poetic genres, so that while the term "verse satire," like "epic," sounds perfectly all right when it is being used to refer to something that exists in the history of literature, it would sound quaint in such a sentence as "I am writing a verse satire." Another reason, less immediate perhaps but more fundamental, is that "satire" is not something we think of very naturally in connection with the idea of "poetry"—not as naturally as we think of "description" or "lyric," for instance.

This is not to say that we utterly cannot see the two as ever being one; but only that when we set out to give someone an idea of what constitutes "poetry," we generally don't use satirical poems as examples. We might refer to an Elizabethan sonnet, an ode by Keats, any number of twentieth-century poems—but not until later would we turn to *Hudibras* or *The Vanity of Human Wishes*. Again, the point is not that we would rule these out, and in fact in the last thirty years or so there have been a number of essays and books which undertake to show that such poems ought to be considered as poetry and not something else.

But our theoretical predispositions about the nature of poetry do in fact rest more comfortably with poems that are not satires, such that many of the same essays and books may, in their anxiety to legitimize satirical poems as true poetry or mythmaking, be put in the position of not especially talking about their intentions and effectiveness as satire. So we are back to the same point: that the idea of poetry and the idea of satire for us convey two different sets of meaning and associated qualities, even it would seem when we try hardest not to let them.

In this connection it is worthwhile to compare our habits of thought with those of the Romantics, most of whom also felt that satiric poems, and more particularly the poems of Pope, were not the best place to look for the definition of poetry itself. But in their case, unlike our own, the pressure of immediate tradition told them to look for it there anyway, whether they felt like it or not. Pope's prestige as a poet —more often as *the* poet—was immense, all through the later years of the eighteenth century and well into the nineteenth; however much you might dislike Pope, you had to concede this about his reputation.

In 1815 Wordsworth wrote that the poems of Pope "still retain their hold upon public estimation,—nay, there is not a passage of descriptive poetry, which at this day finds so many and such ardent admirers." Yet Wordsworth in the next sentence still finds himself hopelessly unable to imagine what it could be like actually to *be* one of those ardent admirers: "Strange to think of an Enthusiast, as may have been the case with thousands, reciting those verses under the cope of a moon-light sky, without having his raptures in the least disturbed by a suspicion of their absurdity!"[1]

Such is the perplexity, so familiar in the period, about Pope, who seemed to stand forth so unarguably as the summing up of English poetry, yet who surely, somehow, could not be *that*. For that reason I think we can scarcely imagine how curious it must have seemed to

Wordsworth to feel that way himself, while at the same time being aware that it would only take "a little previous rummaging" of his memory, as he put it, and he could repeat "several thousand lines of Pope."[2]

What we see in Wordsworth is an answer—perplexed as to historical awareness but in itself a deeply confident answer—to a theoretical question about the nature of poetry that had first arisen in the middle of the eighteenth century. Then, as in Wordsworth's time, the question usually had to do with Pope, but its implications were far more general: Was Pope a poet?

Joseph Warton had asked it in the *Essay on the Genius and Writings of Pope* (1756), claiming that the kind of poetry Pope wrote best was "not the most excellent one of the art."[3] This is a judgment whose terms fall strictly within those of classical genre criticism, and in that respect there is nothing "romantic" about it. What marks it off is that Warton should bother to say something that was supposed to be taken for granted by a classical critic, namely, that didactic and satiric poems are not the highest kinds of poems. When Warton says that the major part of Pope's work is "not of the most poetic species of poetry,"[4] we may rightly suspect that he doesn't simply mean that Pope never wrote an epic or a tragedy.

"Most poetic" implies a basis of value that cuts across generic lines. In classical terms, a poem is what it is by virtue of its "kind"—epic, ode, epistle, satire—each of which has its own intentions, rules of composition and decorum, affective qualities, and instructional or entertainment value. And each of the kinds is equally "poetry." The hint in Warton's *Essay*, however, is that a poem is what it is by virtue of its being poetry and not something else. "Poetry," which in classical criticism was merely the quality or medium common to every genre and not a basis for distinguishing one poem from another, is here seen as a quality not equally present in every genre. Hence we may distinguish poems in terms of the degree to which they are poems, or "poetic," rather than in terms of their generic identity. To the genre critic this would be like saying that the main difference between an oak table and a walnut chair is the wood, since for him the important distinction is between one *kind* of poem and another. Warton, on the other hand, is moving in the direction of making the important distinction that between poetry and prose.

Warton appears to have had a difficult time convincing other people to agree with him about Pope; but Johnson, twenty-five years later, sensed enough force in the question to introduce it into his *Life of Pope*, although only to dismiss it. "After all this," he writes, referring to his own lengthy evaluation of Pope's poetry,

> it is surely superfluous to answer the question that has once been asked, Whether Pope was a poet? otherwise than by asking in return, If Pope be not a poet, where is poetry to be found? To circumscribe poetry by a definition will only shew the narrowness of the definer, though a definition which shall exclude Pope will not easily be made.[5]

Johnson, unlike Warton, sees "poetry" as a name whose meaning is determined, like other nouns, by custom and usage. He puts his finger quite accurately on what was happening when he implies that to ask the question is to seek to circumscribe poetry by a definition.

By Wordsworth's time the desire to redefine poetry as to its true nature, to circumscribe it and set it off from that which only pretended to be poetry, had become clearly articulate. Besides such well-known instances of this as we have in Wordsworth and Coleridge, there is the more aggressive voice of William Lisle Bowles, who in his edition of Pope in 1806 insisted on the intrinsic inferiority of moral, satiric, and even mock-heroic poetry as poetry, and in that took Warton's qualified and decorous criticism a good deal further. And Southey wrote of the Augustans that "whatever praise may be given to them as versifiers, as wits, as reasoners, they may deserve; but versification, and wit, and reason do not constitute poetry."[6]

Byron is the great exception to this attitude, of course; but it is impossible not to see him as an exception proving the rule. It is always wonderful to read him when he is on one of his suicidal campaigns against the Lake poets and the "vulgar and atrocious cant" against Pope, as he called it; or when he talks about how he himself has "shamefully deviated in practice" from the ideal of Pope, but never left off loving it, and would rather see everything he ever wrote turned into lining for a trunk before he would "sacrifice what I firmly believe in as the Christianity of English poetry, the poetry of Pope."[7] But Byron's position communicates its own hopelessness, and one is always aware of it as a conscious objection to the case being made by a school of writers whose influence (Byron undoubtedly sensed) would ultimately be decisive.

It is not really necessary to go into the familiar subject of what, for the Romantics, does constitute poetry, except to say that the Augustans most frequently are disqualified on the score of the artificiality of their subject matter—their focus on the man-made world instead of the natural—and what was taken to be the nonpoetical discursiveness of so much of their poetry. There were other objections, as for instance to the Augustan poetic diction or to the transitory nature of occasional and satiric poems. Underlying this criticism was a feeling that such "poetry" might as well be prose. We see this, for example, in Coleridge's reference to the *Essay on Man* and other poems of that sort as "mere metrical good sense and wit."[8]

While the Romantics did not actually invent the pejorative sense in which the words "verse" and "versifier" can be used, they did use it so often in this sense as to exclude any other meaning. Not every poem, so-called, could be considered "poetry"; and to the extent that it wasn't poetry it belonged, inevitably, to prose, which is the only other category that properly corresponds to poetry. Thus we have prosaic verse, but also poetic prose. Hazlitt writes:

> The question, whether Pope was a poet, has hardly yet been settled, and is hardly worth settling; for if he was not a great poet, he must have been a great prose-writer, that is, he was a great writer of some sort.[9]

In this particular the line of thought on Pope that leads out of the early Romantic criticism seems to run in a natural progression through Hazlitt and finally to Arnold in his celebrated resolution of the whole question by denominating Dryden and Pope "classics of our prose."

Johnson would say that this definition of poetry shows its own narrowness; which it does, of course, in that certain types of verse that used to be called "poetry" now must be called something else: either "verse" in the pejorative sense or, more dramatically, "prose." This has proved to be a lasting reorientation in our view of poetry, formulated perhaps in other and less obvious terms in our own time but substantially the same. We still talk about the "prose sense" of a poem as if that could have nothing to do with the true being of the poem, and we still would seem to feel that discursive clarity is a value that can define the quality of prose, perhaps, but not poetry.

In the late eighteenth and early nineteenth century, then, the province of what is called true poetry simply shrinks, though we must suppose that it makes up in depth what it loses in extensiveness. The tendency was to allow the province to include human feeling but not human wit, natural imagery but not artificial, meditative and symbolic modes of expression but not discursive or dialectical. Outside the province lay satires, history poems, verse essays, imitations, epistles, mock-epics, realistic and moral fables, theatrical prologues and epilogues, epitaphs and epigrams. Not that all such poetry suddenly stopped being written, although eventually much of it did, but only that a poet who chose to write this kind of poetry ran the extra risk of being considered less than truly a poet.

Along with these developments is an increasing emphasis on the theoretical distinction between poetry and prose. This is perhaps predictable at a time when prose is in effect "taking over" some of the territory otherwise occupied by poetry: in narrative literature (the novel), in literary criticism and essay writing (essays in prose rather than verse), and in satire (again, largely in the novel).[10]

The Augustans had recognized a distinction between poetry and prose, certainly, but seldom in absolute terms. Usually, in fact, we have to look hard to find any reference to the distinction other than implicitly, in remarks that do not directly bear on the subject. Dryden on one memorable occasion talks about how his thoughts come crowding in on him so fast that his only problem as a writer is in deciding whether "to run them into verse or to give them the other harmony of prose."[11] In one way of looking at it, this is the heresy of paraphrase in reverse, where the heretic is not the ingenuous classroom reader but the poet himself. For Dryden seems to be saying that when he writes poetry what he basically does is embody a "prose sense" in verse.[12]

Dryden conceives of the distinction between poetry and prose in terms of what the writer is at liberty to do with each, without making special claims for one against the other. Elsewhere in the Augustan period we find the concept of "proper style" as the basis for the distinction: in *An Epistle to a Friend concerning Poetry* (1700), a verse essay, Samuel Wesley speaks of poetry as requiring "strong figures" and prose, a "neat plainness."[13] Sometimes too the distinction seems to lie in prosody, the idea being that poetry is a more "measured" style of prose. The point is that these various distinctions are capable of being resolved into questions of decorum and intention, seldom with any particular prejudice to either "harmony," poetry or prose, at the expense of the other. In any event, it never seems very necessary to make a distinction.

The distinction begins to acquire some importance as a problem of criticism later in the eighteenth century, as the older genre-distinctions command less attention. Significantly, the post–Augustan writers and critics confront the question more directly than had commonly been the case. More often too the characteristics they cite as distinctive of poetry are likely to be drawn only from certain genres of poetry, especially the heroic, descriptive, and lyric. For Bishop Lowth, poetry differs from prose in speaking "the language of the passions."[14] For Erasmus Darwin, the difference is that "the poet writes principally to the eye; the prose writer uses more abstracted terms."[15]

Now it is possible to see all of these changes—the more restricted definition of poetry, the increased awareness of or insistence upon a difference between poetry and prose—as consistent with classical criticism. That is, these are shifts in theory which are at least potentially within the terms of classical criticism, as opposed to something like Coleridge's concept of the imagination, which is not. The real change consists in a novel exploitation of this potential for what I would call a political purpose: that of establishing certain literary styles and subject materials as the exclusive property of poetry.

How does satiric poetry fit into this picture I have been reviewing? First and most obviously, the traditional practice of writing satire in verse is now, in the latter half of the eighteenth century, exposed to a degree of doubt as to its own legitimacy. If it were possible to speak of a literary genre as having an identity crisis, or having an inferiority complex, that would accurately characterize the state of satiric poetry between the death of Pope and the beginning of the nineteenth century. What this means in plainer terms is that many of these poems lack confidence as satire.

This quality manifests itself in a number of different ways. Generally speaking, as I have tried to show, post–Augustan verse satire moves away from the impersonal point of view of heroic satire, developing instead a strong sense of limitation in the satirist's perspective on his subject. At the same time the satirist becomes conspicuously self-conscious. The emotional tone of this satire is characteristically much mellower and more indulgent than in Augustan satire—a change that blurs the generic line between satire and humor. And somewhat later in the period we encounter, principally in Peter Pindar and in Byron, the tone of self-deprecating irony that is positively fatal to the credibility of a poem as serious satire.

Indirectly at least, all of these changes constitute a retreat from the assumptions of the genre as it had been practiced by the Augustans. What is of more special interest in this chapter, however, are those aspects of post–Augustan satire which reflect directly on the question of the relationship between satire and poetry. This puts us upon the task of looking at the idea of satire as it is represented in the satiric poems themselves, and also at the role of "poetry," taken in its newer sense, in those poems.

One would expect the changing conception of poetry to have brought about a reduction in the number of satires written in verse form. And while this is definitely what happens in the long run, nevertheless during the last half of the eighteenth century there is not really any falling off of that sort. We do hear it said of Thomas Blacklock, a minor poet of the period, that although he was "extremely sensible to what he thought ill usage . . . his resentment was always confined to a few satirical verses, which were generally burnt soon after."[16] For most of the satirists, however, the old habit of publishing continued in force.

Yet a special pressure does bear on the genre. It may appear as a more skeptical attitude toward the serious pretensions of satire. A satirist like Cleveland can write, confidently and unreflectingly,

> Come keen *Iambicks*, with your Badgers feet,
> And Badger-like, bite till your teeth do meet.[17]

Or Pope,

> Come on then Satire! gen'ral, unconfin'd,
> Spread thy broad wing, and sowze on all the Kind.[18]

The post–Augustan writer's allusions to satire, to what it is and what it can do, however, often incorporate a certain feeling of doubt as to whether the old pretensions can really be fulfilled. So with Cowper,

> Yet what can satire, whether grave or gay?
> It may correct a foible, may chastise
> The freaks of fashion, regulate the dress,
> Retrench a sword-blade, or displace a patch;
> But where are its sublimer trophies found?
> What vice has it subdu'd? whose heart reclaim'd
> By rigour, or whom laugh'd into reform? [19]

In those instances where the satirist makes a serious reference to the Muse of Satire, the effect is a very self-conscious one. Many verse satires have this quality in common, of course, just as most verse satire is defensive and self-apologetic from to time—it is in Horace and Juvenal, in Marston and Oldham and Rochester, in Young and Pope. The distinction between Augustan and post–Augustan satire in this respect is one of emphasis and degree: beginning with Pope's later satires, and in the period after that, from Churchill to Byron, the level of self-consciousness about "Satire" is extremely high: in Churchill's poem *The Author*, for example, we are introduced to a supposedly hypocritical aristocrat who maintains, or pretends to maintain, that satire has no real effect on anybody and that "within the hour, / Left to herself, she dies . . ." (ll. 202–3). The poet answers, over-reacting violently to the question:

> Dissembling Wretch! hence to the Stoic school,
> And there amongst thy breth'ren play the fool,

> There, unrebuk'd, these wild, vain doctrines preach;
> Lives there a Man, whom Satire cannot reach?
> Lives there a Man, who calmly can stand by,
> And see his conscience ripp'd with steady eye?
>
> [ll. 211–16]

The odd thing about this, though, is that in 1763, when the poem was written, these were comonplace doctrines, not wild or vain in the least. There is the same note of anxiety about the threatened position of satire in Canning and Frere's *New Morality*, which observes nostalgically that "venial vices, in a milder age, / Could rouse the warmth of Pope's satiric rage . . ." then demands,

> But say,—indignant does the Muse retire,
> Her shrine deserted, and extinct its fire?
> No pious hand to feed the sacred flame,
> No raptured soul a poet's charge to claim? [20]

In some cases, the traditional pretensions of satire will themselves become the subject of ironic criticism or even ridicule, and we have something comparable to the convention of the satirist–satirized. In Peter Pindar's *One Thousand Seven Hundred and Ninety-Six*, there is a dialogue between a would-be satirical poet named Tom and the author himself, who brings a feeling of world-weariness to bear on the young poet's satirical zeal. The overall effect, as in the following excerpt, is to diminish and "contain" the whole idea of satire as a scourge of villainy: Tom says,

> Arm'd with the lightning's pointed fire, my pen,
> Brand thou the daring fronts of shameless men;
> Drag thou, my arm, black Guilt to open day!—
> Such are my projects: how d'ye like them, pray?

Peter replies,

> Nobly resolved; a pious resolution,
> Would Fortune kindly crown the execution.
> But Pitt despised the execrating noise
> Of men and women, hooting girls and boys;

> Smiled at the rude salutes of stones and mire
> That discomposed his curls and gay attire
>
> .  .  .  .  .  .  .  .  .  .  .  .
>
> Safe 'mid the windings of his brazen tower,
> Too well a Minister discerns his power;
> With high contempt he bids their fury flow,
> And mocks the pop-guns of the World below . . .[21]

This movement toward a more literal-minded interpretation of the classic pretensions of satire is one of the most interesting post–Augustan trends. It results, quite obviously, in a virtual rejection of the pretensions, since to take any such stylized attitude literally is to expose it as mere convention. In his poem *On Ridicule* (1743), for example, William Whitehead argues that satire simply doesn't work the way it claims to—that vicious men aren't afraid of it, that fools can't understand it, and that good men are sometimes injured by it. Byron takes a similarly realistic (but personal) approach to the psychology of satire at one point in *Beppo*:

> I fear I have a little turn for satire,
> And yet methinks the older that one grows
> Inclines us more to laugh than scold, though laughter
> Leaves us so doubly serious shortly after.
>
> [st. 79]

The pretensions of satire, however unrealistic they may be, traditionally give the genre a basis for its conventional existence, that is, its existence as a genre. Other, nameless forces in the human psychology no doubt form the basis for its existence in reality; but in order to continue in a legitimate generic capacity, the verse satire depends upon a more or less uncritical acceptance of its pretensions. When these are questioned seriously, as they are during this period, the genre simply begins to seem unnecessary or beside the point. Shelley's "Fragment of a Satire on Satire" (1820) can be seen as the logical if not actual culmination of this tendency:

> If Satire's scourge could wake the slumbering hounds
> Of Conscience, or erase the deeper wounds,

The leprous scars of callous Infamy;
If it could make the present not to be,
Or charm the dark past never to have been,
Or turn regret to hope; who that has seen
What Southey is and was, would not exclaim,
'Lash on!'

But satire cannot do any of these things. It would be better, Shelley goes on,

If any friend would take Southey some day,
And tell him, in a country walk alone,
Softening harsh words with friendship's gentle tone,
How incorrect his public conduct is,
And what men think of it, 'twere not amiss.[22]

Later eighteenth-century verse satire takes account of the changing concept of "poetry" chiefly in two ways: either by actually being at times "poetic" in the sense in which that term excludes satire, or by introducing references, sometimes hostile or contemptuous, to "poetry" as it is coming to be defined during the period.

As to the first of these points, frequently the satiric poetry of the period consists partly of "satire," partly of "poetry," each independent of the other: that is, neither element can really be seen as helping to fulfill the purposes of the other, as certain "poetic" qualities in Pope's satire, such as description and imagery, have a satirical function.

In Chapter 4 I gave some instances of this effect, in particular the first stanza of Burns's *The Holy Fair* and Thomas Warton's satire *Newmarket*, where the satirical poem becomes for a time a purely descriptive, hence purely "poetic" poem. Or if the individual satire does not itself actually become "poetic" in this way, there are still those related cases in which the two types of poetry, satiric and lyrical, are brought together or juxtaposed so as to create much the same effect, that of satire losing its generic integrity as satire, offering to become some other kind of poetry. So it is with Peter Pindar's habit of mixing seriously intended lyric odes with his satiric ones, or the likewise seriously intended lyric poems that Gifford wrote to be included in the footnotes to the *Maeviad* as a kind of alternative to the awful Della Cruscan poetry.

One thinks too of the passages of lyrical poetry in *Don Juan*. In that work the essential connection between the lyric poetry and the satire, whatever it is, cannot be understood in generic terms; we can seek the connection somewhere else, perhaps in the concept of the poem as a dramatization of the poet's personality, but in any case we won't find any traditional genre by which both elements, the lyric and the satiric, may be subsumed and thus related to each other.

In general, then, one of the distinguishing marks of post–Augustan satire is a considerable degree of generic confusion. It appears in Churchill, where the question so often arises whether some poem of his (e.g., *The Rosciad, The Ghost*) ought to be called a satire; or in Cowper, in a poem such as *The Task*, which could not be defined as a satire and yet contains satire; and the confusion is likewise apparent in what I have just been describing as the tendency for some satire in the period to be sympathetically receptive to the infusion of lyrical or descriptive styles of poetry that carry with them no satiric value.

In other instances of post–Augustan satire, however, such styles may be given an unsympathetic reception—may be introduced into the satire, that is, but only as parody or otherwise as an object of scorn. Here the effect is not that of a genre showing confusion about what it is supposed to consist of, but instead that of a genre protecting itself against rival kinds of poetry. One notices that from about 1780 onward verse satire deals increasingly with the subject of literature, especially the type of literature that can be sneeringly referred to as "poesy." Churchill had occasionally written in this vein: "*Me*, thus uncouth, thus ev'ry way unfit / For *pacing* poesy, and *ambling* wit . . ."[23]

There is nothing new in satires on the abuses of literature, of course, but one important distinction can be made between the Augustan and post–Augustan examples of such satire: in *Mac Flecknoe* and Rochester's *Allusion to Horace*, in Swift's *On Poetry: A Rapsody* and in Pope's countless excursions against bad poetry, the emphasis falls always on the writing as a reflection of the writer—his witlessness and bungling execution, his ignorance, his dullness. But the later satirists give their attention more exclusively to certain *kinds* of poetry which they dislike, as when Robert Lloyd criticizes Miltonic imitation in his epistle *On Rhyme* (1762), or when Gifford attacks the Della Cruscan school of poetry in *The Baviad* and *The Maeviad*. And again, more brilliantly, there is the satire on current literature in the *Anti-Jacobin* and in Byron's *English Bards and Scotch Reviewers*, which preeminently ridicules the new styles of poetry. Byron's concern in that poem lies partly in defending against the overthrow of one conception of poetry by another. This is perhaps more vividly illustrated by comparing *English Bards* to the *Dunciad*, in that all of the writers that Pope derides, with one or two exceptions, have failed to survive, while Byron in that respect is hardly so successful as a prophet. Besides the obvious case of Wordsworth and Coleridge, who manage to survive despite Byron, there are those writers who do not survive but whom Byron sets forth as examples of "neglected genius"—Campbell, Rogers, Gifford, Sotheby, Macneil—a contention that now seems terribly perverse unless we consider that these are writers whose poetry harks back to Pope, and that this, rather than their genius as individual poets, is what brings Byron to beat his drum for them.

The attacks on modern literature in the *Anti-Jacobin* are mostly in the form of parody, such as *The Friend of Humanity and the Knife-grinder*, which hits off Southey so incomparably. There is no widespread or consistent use of parody in the early part of the century, but beginning around 1780 the form suddenly seems to prosper. Soame Jenyns has a parody of the Pindaric Ode in 1780, and a few years later there are the *Probationary Odes for the Laureatship* by the *Rolliad* writers (1785 and many editions thereafter). These pretended to be poems submitted in candidacy for the laureatship vacated by William Whitehead's death, and they included parodies of Macpherson, William Mason (as a descriptive poet, of course), and the Wartons, among others.

Parody becomes the most distinctive form that satire takes in the nineteenth century.[24] Satire, in fact, would almost seem to have attached itself to other styles of poetry so as to give over its serious pretensions and generic autonomy almost completely. One sees this particularly in the good humored tone of many of the nineteenth-century parodies. *The Vision of Judgment*, like the hostile parodies in the *Anti-Jacobin*, is an exception to this point. But the general direction is toward toleration, as for example in James and Horatio Smith's

*Rejected Addresses* (1812) and William Combe's parody of William Gilpin, the *Tour of Dr. Syntax in Search of the Picturesque* (1812).[25] These give the impression that the writer assumes that the thing he parodies has as good a claim to existence as his parody of it.

Verse satire does not entirely cease to exist in the nineteenth century. There are dozens of political satires, especially up until passage of the 1832 reform measures. But the point remains that the satire in verse appears to have sustained itself only by predicating its existence on something else—politics, or other types of poetry. I think this can be judged as a change that is progressively consistent with the changes that take place in the form during the last half of the eighteenth century.

In the Renaissance, and throughout the seventeenth and most of the eighteenth centuries, the satire in verse form is a thoroughly familiar type of literature; afterward it is not, and might reasonably be said to have lapsed indefinitely. In the transition between eighteenth- and nineteenth-century literature, then, something happens that had not happened before, and in explaining what this is I have emphasized the matter of poetic genre and the redefinition of poetry. Obviously there may be other reasons: the growth and popularity of sentimental literature, presupposing a wider interest in the spirit of sympathetic fellow-feeling at the expense of the unsympathetic emotions of satire; changing cultural attitudes, and a boredom with the ideal, so passionately set forth by the Augustans, of a civilization of rational good sense; and even perhaps the increasingly republican tone of politics. Such purely social or cultural or political changes as these might possibly explain why "satire" in the broader adjectival sense—the so-called Spirit of Satire—could disappear from literature at some particular moment of history. But of course this is not exactly what happened, or has happened, since satire in prose form makes at least a respectable showing in the nineteenth century, particularly if we take into account the satiric element in the novel, and a very strong showing in the twentieth. It is verse satire that goes out of business, and so in looking for an explanation of this fact, one is naturally led to consider satire strictly in respect of its being (or not being) a type of verse.

In this respect, then, the history of verse satire after Pope is the history of a genre trying to accommodate itself to the shift in ideas about what makes a poem. The subject of verse satire, according to Juvenal, is "whatever men do." Dryden and Pope, who think of themselves as poets, very confidently accept this formula. But in the next century most of the writers who take up society and the doings of men as their subject are novelists. The poets are interested in other things. The effect, though perhaps overstated for the emphasis, is to give the would-be writer a choice: either to be a poet and not a satirist, or to be a satirist and not a poet—but not both.

# Notes

ALL OF THE quotations from Churchill in this book are taken from *The Poetical Works of Charles Churchill*, ed. Douglas Grant (Oxford: The Clarendon Press, 1956). For Dryden, Pope, Cowper, Burns, and Byron I have used the following standard texts throughout: *The Poems of John Dryden*, ed. James Kinsley, 4 vols. (Oxford: The Clarendon Press, 1958); *The Poems of Alexander Pope*, ed. John Butt (New Haven: Yale University Press, 1963); *The Poetical Works of William Cowper*, ed. H. S. Milford (4th ed.; Oxford: Oxford University Press, 1934); *The Poems and Songs of Robert Burns*, ed. James Kinsley, 3 vols. (Oxford: The Clarendon Press, 1968); *The Works of Lord Byron: Poetry*, ed. E. H. Coleridge, 7 vols. (London: John Murray, 1898–1904).

## INTRODUCTION

1. I am as uneasy as anyone about using such terms as "Augustan" or "post–Augustan" to designate literary periods. I have used them anyway in this book, hoping to excuse myself on the grounds of convenience: such alternative ways of referring to my subject material as "satires written between 1750 and 1800" seem hopelessly awkward. "Augustan" and "post–Augustan" admittedly have an evaluative significance that may be misleading, but within reason they probably can be allowed to have such a significance. That there are in fact general, though not invariable or exclusive differences between earlier and later eighteenth-century literature, suggests to me that the terms are not utterly without value so long as they are applied only where the occasion requires no more exactness or discrimination than they can provide.

2. *An Epistle to Mr. Colman, Written in the Year 1756*, in *The Poetical Works of Robert Lloyd, A.M.*, ed. W. Kenrick, 2 vols. (London, 1774), 1: 166–67.

3. "The Stretching of Augustan Satire: Charles Churchill's 'Dedication' to Warburton," *Journal of English and Germanic Philology* 72 (1973):360–77.

4. *The Works of the English Poets, from Chaucer to Cowper*, ed. Alexander

Chalmers, 21 vols. (London, 1810), and *The Works of the British Poets*, ed. Robert Anderson, 13 vols. (London, 1795). The parts of the Chalmers anthology that include minor poets unavailable in modern editions have been usefully brought together and reissued as *Minor English Poets, 1660–1780*, ed. David P. French, 10 vols. (New York: Arno, 1967).

5. *PMLA* 85(1970):260–67. In addition to this, the lengthy introduction to Sherard Vines's *Georgian Satirists*, pp. 1–54, makes useful generalizations about the recurrent topics of the satire of this period, as well as giving a lively picture of many of the relevant historical particulars. Other studies in which there is some attempt to survey post–Augustan satire as a whole include C. W. Previté-Orton, *Political Satire in English Poetry* (Cambridge: Cambridge University Press, 1910), pp. 129–65; Hugh Walker, *English Satire and Satirists* (London: J. M. Dent & Sons, 1925), pp. 222–77; and James Sutherland, fleetingly in his *English Satire* (Cambridge: Cambridge University Press, 1958), pp. 65–78. Previté-Orton is not always reliable in matters of fact, but Walker's account is very sensible and contains some worthwhile general observations. For an essay on possible underlying causes of the decline of satire, see Andrew M. Wilkinson, "The Decline of English Verse Satire in the Middle Years of the Eighteenth Century," *Review of English Studies*, n.s. 3(1952):223–33. On Churchill himself, Raymond J. Smith's *Charles Churchill* (Boston: Twayne, 1977) is particularly useful for its account of Churchill as a political poet.

6. *Journal of English and Germanic Philology* 66(1967):333–46.

### CHAPTER 1

1. *Spectator*, no. 297 (9 February 1712).

2. Life of Thomson, in *Lives of the English Poets*, ed. G. Birkbeck Hill, 3 vols. (Oxford: The Clarendon Press, 1905), 3:299–300.

3. *A Discourse concerning the Original and Progress of Satire* (1692/3), in *Of Dramatic Poesy and other Critical Essays*, ed. George Watson, 2 vols. (London: J. M. Dent & Sons, 1962), 2:144–46.

4. "The Structural Design of the Formal Verse Satire," *Philological Quarterly* 21(1942):368–84.

5. *A Tale of a Tub*, ed. A. C. Guthkelch and D. Nichol Smith (2nd ed.; Oxford: The Clarendon Press, 1958), p. 144.

6. Ibid., p. 4.

7. Charles Churchill, *Independence* (1764), ll. 219–25.

8. Ll. 1–6, in *The Complete Works of Thomas Chatterton*, ed. Donald S. Taylor, 2 vols. (Oxford: The Clarendon Press, 1970), 1:412.

9. Ll. 87–88, in *Complete Works*, ed. Taylor, 1:414.

10. *Complete Works*, ed. Taylor, 1:504.

11. *Epistle to Arbuthnot*, ll. 5–10.

12. *The Poetical Works of David Garrick*, 2 vols. (London, 1785), 1:38–39.

13. *The Works of Peter Pindar, Esq.*, 5 vols. (London, 1812), 1:474. This is the best of the collected editions, though far from a complete one.

14. Ibid., 1:53–54.

15. *The Task* (1785), bk. 2, ll. 414–18.

16. *Critical Review* 16(1763):335–38.

17. *Monthly Review* 27(1762):316.

18. Ibid., 29(1763):397.

19. *Gotham*, bk. 2, l. 192.

20. This is in *The Ghost*, bk. 4, ll. 813–62.

21. *Kew Gardens*, ll. 761–62, in *Complete Works*, ed. Taylor, 1:533.

22. From the "Advertisement" to the poem.

23. "An Introductory Letter" (added to the fifth edition of the poem, 1798), in *The Pursuits of Literature. A Satirical Poem in Four Dialogues, with Notes* (14th ed.; London, 1808), pp. 10–11.

### CHAPTER 2

1. Cf. Horace, *Satires*, bk. 2, sat. 1; Persius, *Satires*, sat. 1; and Juvenal, *Satires*, sat. 1, ll. 150–71. For a discussion of the satiric apologia in Latin literature, see L. R. Shero, "The Satirist's Apologia," *Classical Studies*, ser. 2, University of Wisconsin Studies in Language and Literature, no. 15(1922): 148–67. For a useful presentation on the apologia in the English Restoration and eighteenth-century period, see P. K. Elkin, *The Augustan Defense of Satire* (Oxford: The Clarendon Press, 1973).

2. Ll. 57–60, in *Poems on Affairs of State*, gen. ed. George deF. Lord, 7 vols. (New Haven: Yale University Press, 1963–75), vol. 2, ed. Elias F. Mengel, Jr., pp. 19–22.

3. *Rochester's 'Poems on Several Occasions,'* ed. James Thorpe (Princeton: Princeton University Press, 1950), p. 45.

4. Life of Pope, in *Lives of the English Poets*, ed. G. Birkbeck Hill, 3 vols. (Oxford: The Clarendon Press, 1905), 3:243.

5. Consider, as one example out of many, Ben Jonson's reference to "the impossibility of any man's being the good poet without first being a good man" (in the Preface to *Volpone*).

6. *Of Dramatic Poesy and other Critical Essays*, ed. George Watson, 2 vols. (London: J. M. Dent & Sons, 1962), 2:125.

7. *Tatler*, no. 242 (26 October 1710).

8. See especially *Spectator*, nos. 169 (13 September 1711) and 249 (15 December 1711). For an important study dealing in large part with satire and the concept of good nature, see Stuart Tave, *The Amiable Humorist* (Chicago: University of Chicago Press, 1960).

9. *Spectator*, no. 35 (10 April 1711).

10. Ibid., no. 209 (30 October 1711).

11. Tave, *The Amiable Humorist*, p. 23.

12. Reprinted in *The Gentleman's Magazine* 9(March 1739):136–37.

13. See, in addition to Tave, Andrew M. Wilkinson, "The Rise of English Verse Satire in the Eighteenth Century," *Review of English Studies* 34(1953): 97–108; the companion article, "The Decline of English Verse Satire in the Middle Years of the Eighteenth Century," *Review of English Studies*, n.s. 3

(1952):223–33; and Elkin, *The Augustan Defense of Satire*, pp. 44–70.

14. *The Inspector*, no. 136, in the collected edition, 2 vols. (London, 1753), 2:252.

15. *A Poetical Translation of the Works of Horace*, 4 vols. (2nd ed.; London, 1747), vol. 3, pp. vii–viii.

16. *The Prose Works of Jonathan Swift*, ed. Herbert Davis, 14 vols. (Oxford: Basil Blackwell, 1939–68), 12:34.

17. Thomas Cooke, *Tales, Epistles, Odes, Fables, &c* . . . (London, 1729), p. 139.

18. See Mary Claire Randolph, "Candour in Eighteenth-Century Satire," *Review of English Studies* 20(1944):45–62.

19. *An Inquiry concerning Virtue or Merit* (1699), bk. 1, pt. 3, sect. 1, in *Characteristics of Men, Manners, Opinions, Times, etc.*, ed. John M. Robertson, 2 vols. (London: Grant Richards, 1900), 1:260.

20. *The Censor*, no. 2 (13 April 1715), in the collected edition, 2 vols. (London, 1717), 1:12.

21. *The Rhetorical World of Augustan Humanism* (Oxford: The Clarendon Press, 1965), p. 20.

22. *The Collected Poems of Christopher Smart*, ed. Norman Callan, 2 vols. (London: Routledge & Kegan Paul, 1949), 1:164.

23. *The Poems and Miscellaneous Compositions of Paul Whitehead*, ed. Capt. Edward Thompson (London, 1777), pp. 91–92.

24. Ibid., p. 93.

25. Ibid., pp. 94–95.

26. For a fuller commentary on this poem, see below, chap. 5.

27. Ed. Edith J. Morley (London: Longmans & Co., 1918), p. 24.

28. *Monthly Review* 24(1761):342.

29. For more on the subjectivism in Pope, as well as Swift, see G. K. Hunter, "The 'Romanticism' of Pope's Horace," *Essays in Criticism* 10(1960):390–404, and Ronald Paulson, *The Fictions of Satire* (Baltimore: The Johns Hopkins University Press, 1967), pp. 185–210.

30. For instance:

> Prose-driving dunces, waddling fools in rhime,
> Scoundrels of ev'ry kind, by vengeance led,
> Spit forth your venom, poison all our clime,
> Churchill, who scourg'd you to your holes, is dead!

This was reprinted, alas, in the *New Foundling Hospital for Wit*, 6 vols. (London, 1784), 4:85. In this connection see also Joseph M. Beatty, Jr., "Churchill's Influence on Minor Eighteenth Century Satirists," *PMLA* 42(1927):162–76. But cf. Robert C. Whitford, "Gleanings of Churchill Bibliography," *Modern Language Notes* 43(1928):30–34.

31. Most notably for Chatterton and Cowper. As to the latter, see Morris Golden, "Churchill's Literary Influence on Cowper," *Journal of English and Germanic Philology* 58(1959):655–65.

32. *An Epistle to Mr. Colman*, in *The Poetical Works of Robert Lloyd, A.M.*, ed. W. Kenrick, 2 vols. (London, 1774), 1:165.

33. Ibid., 1:172, 179.
34. Ibid., 1:130.
35. Ibid., 2:50.
36. *Kew Gardens*, ll. 557–64, in *The Complete Works of Thomas Chatterton*, ed. Donald S. Taylor, 2 vols. (Oxford: The Clarendon Press, 1970), 1:528.
37. Ibid., ll. 388–94, in *Complete Works*, ed. Taylor, 1:523.
38. *The Poetical Works of the Late Christopher Anstey, Esq.*, ed. John Anstey (London, 1808), pp. 123, 124.
39. The full title of the piece is "Appendix: Containing the Author's Conversation with His Bookseller, &c." (Ibid., pp. 167–73).
40. Ll. 1–2, 5–6; ll. 29–30; ll. 107–10, in *Satirical Poems Published Anonymously by William Mason with Notes by Horace Walpole*, ed. Paget Toynbee (Oxford: The Clarendon Press, 1926), pp. 74–79.
41. Ll. 28–41, in *Satirical Poems*, ed. Toynbee, p. 105.
42. *Expostulatory Odes to a Great Duke and a Little Lord* (1789), Ode 9, in *The Works of Peter Pindar, Esq.*, 5 vols. (London, 1812), 2:235.
43. *The Pursuits of Literature. A Satirical Poem in Four Dialogues, with Notes* (14th ed.; London, 1808), dial. 1, l. 48, note "m."
44. *The Works of Peter Pindar*, 2:45.
45. Ibid., 2:461.
46. Ibid., 2:294.
47. For some specific historical references, though unhelpful conclusions, see R. C. Whitford, "Juvenal in England, 1750–1800," *Philological Quarterly* 7(1928):9–16.
48. Whitford, "Juvenal in England," p. 16.
49. See above, Introduction, n. 5.
50. Ll. 29–42. This and the subsequent quotations from the *Anti-Jacobin* satires are taken from the text in *Poetry of the Anti-Jacobin*, ed. L. Rice-Oxley (Oxford: Basil Blackwell, 1924).

CHAPTER 3

1. *Absalom and Achitophel*, ll. 198–99.
2. *Epilogue to the Satires*, ll. 242–45.
3. *Personification in Eighteenth-Century English Poetry* (New York: King's Crown Press, 1955), p. 3. See also the important studies by Bertrand H. Bronson, "Personification Reconsidered," *ELH* 14(1947):163–77; and Earl R. Wasserman, "The Inherent Values of Eighteenth Century Personification," *PMLA* 65(1950):435–63.
4. Cf. the way in which Maynard Mack showed Pope's expressions often to resemble metaphor without actually being metaphor: "'Wit and Poetry and Pope': Some Observations on his Imagery," *Pope and his Contemporaries. Essays Presented to George Sherburn*, ed. James L. Clifford and Louis Landa (Oxford: The Clarendon Press, 1949), pp. 20–40.
5. *The Works of Samuel Johnson*, 11 vol. (Oxford, 1825), 5:27.
6. Bk. 3, chap. 10, para. 15. This and the subsequent quotations from the

*Essay* are taken from the edition of A. C. Fraser, 2 vols. (Oxford: The Clarendon Press, 1894).

7. Pt. 5, sect. 4. This and the subsequent quotations from the *Enquiry* are taken from the edition of J. T. Boulton (London: Routledge & Kegan Paul, 1958).

8. *Spectator*, no. 416 (27 June 1712).

9. *Essay on the Genius and Writings of Pope* (4th ed., 1782), in *Eighteenth-Century Critical Essays*, ed. Scott Elledge, 2 vols. (Ithaca, N.Y.: Cornell University Press, 1961), 2:756.

10. Chapin, *Personification in Eighteenth-Century English Poetry*, pp. 47–48. The quotations are Anna Letitia Barbauld's, from her edition of Collins, *The Poetical Works* (London, 1797), p. xxiv.

11. Chapin, *Personification in Eighteenth-Century English Poetry*, p. 31.

12. *The Prophecy of Famine*, ll. 85–86.

13. *The Poetical Works of Robert Lloyd, A.M.*, ed. W. Kenrick, 2 vols. (London, 1774), 1:132–46.

14. *Revaluation: Tradition and Development in English Poetry* (London: Chatto & Windus, 1936), p. 118.

15. *Purity of Diction in English Verse* (London: Chatto & Windus, 1952), p. 46.

16. "Of the Standard of Taste," in *Four Dissertations* (1757), reprinted in *Eighteenth-Century Critical Essays*, ed. Elledge, 2:812–13.

17. L. 578, in *The Complete Works of Thomas Chatterton*, ed. Donald S. Taylor, 2 vols. (Oxford: The Clarendon Press, 1970), 1:528.

18. Ll. 71–72, in *Complete Works*, ed. Taylor, 1:437.

19. *Expostulation* (1782), ll. 298–303.

20. *The Dunciad*, bk. 4, ll. 649–50.

21. *Honour: A Satire* (1747), in *The Poems and Miscellaneous Compositions of Paul Whitehead*, ed. Capt. Edward Thompson (London, 1777), p. 107.

22. *Don Juan*, canto 10, st. 68.

23. *The New Foundling Hospital for Wit*, 6 vols. (London, 1784), 1: 266–78.

24. Ode 2 of *Odes of Condolence* (1792), in *The Works of Peter Pindar, Esq.*, 5 vols. (London, 1812), 3:96.

25. *The Defence* (1769), ll. 13–15, in *Complete Works*, 1:421.

26. Ll. 81–96. This and the subsequent quotations from *New Morality* are taken from the text in *Poetry of the Anti-Jacobin*, ed. L. Rice-Oxley (Oxford: Basil Blackwell, 1924).

CHAPTER 4

1. *Essay on Criticism*, ll. 297–300.

2. John Philips, *A Satyr Against Hypocrites* (London, 1655), in Augustan Reprint Society publication no. 38 (Los Angeles: William Andrews Clark Memorial Library, 1953), p. 7.

3. *A Common Observation* (1645), in Hyder E. Rollins, *Cavalier and Puritan* (New York: New York University Press, 1923), p. 158.

4. See Wimsatt's essay, "The Substantive Level," in *The Verbal Icon* (Lexington, Ky.: University of Kentucky Press, 1954), pp. 133–51.

5. Ll. 12–21, in *The Complete Poems of John Wilmot, Earl of Rochester*, ed. David M. Vieth (New Haven: Yale University Press, 1968), p. 95.

6. *The Poems of John Dryden*, ed. James Kinsley, 4 vols. (Oxford: The Clarendon Press, 1958), 3:1036–37.

7. As to content, the subject has been systematically treated in Ronald Paulson, *The Fictions of Satire* (Baltimore: The Johns Hopkins University Press, 1967).

8. *Love of Fame, the Universal Passion*, Satire 2 (1725), ll. 73–84, in *The Poetical Works of Edward Young*, ed. J. Mitford, 2 vols. ("Aldine edition"; London, 1858), 2:71.

9. Gay, *Fables* (1738), Fable 1, l. 49, in *John Gay: Poetry and Prose*, ed. Vinton A. Dearing with Charles E. Beckwith, 2 vols. (Oxford: The Clarendon Press, 1974), 2:382.

10. Text from *The Penguin Book of Satirical Verse*, ed. Edward Lucie-Smith (Baltimore: Penguin Books, 1967), p. 105.

11. *Love of Fame, the Universal Passion*, Satire 5 (1727), l. 432, in *Poetical Works*, ed. Mitford, 2:109.

12. *The Works of Richard Owen Cambridge, Esq.*, ed. George Owen Cambridge (London, 1803), p. 83.

13. Ll. 23–24, 31–38, in *The Poetical Works of the Late Thomas Warton, B.D.*, ed. Richard Mant, 2 vols. (5th ed.; Oxford, 1802), 2:166–68.

14. *The Lousiad*, Canto 4 (1792), in *The Works of Peter Pindar, Esq.*, 5 vols. (London, 1812), 1:282–83.

15. *The Poetical Works of Robert Lloyd, A.M.*, ed. W. Kenrick, 2 vols. (London, 1774), 1:35.

16. *The Poetical Works of the Late Christopher Anstey, Esq.*, ed. John Anstey (London, 1808), p. 86.

17. *The Works of Peter Pindar*, 3:112.

18. Ibid., 1:281–82.

19. For a similar use of character and point of view, see *The Royal Visit to Exeter* (1795), a verse epistle in dialect supposed to have been written by a farmer, "John Ploughshare," in *The Works of Peter Pindar*, 3:465–83.

20. *The Works of the Right Honourable Sir Chas. Hanbury Williams, K.B.*, ed. Edward Jeffrey, 3 vols. (London, 1822), 1:157–58.

21. It might be noted that this distinction is taken up as a topic of analysis in M. K. Joseph's *Byron the Poet* (London: Victor Gollancz, 1964), pp. 194–202.

CHAPTER 5

1. *Anatomy of Criticism* (Princeton: Princeton University Press, 1957), p. 40.

2. *Rump: Or an Exact Collection Of the Choycest Poems and Songs . . . from Anno 1639. to Anno 1661*, 2 vols. (London, 1662), 1:53.

3. Ibid., 1:53.

4. James Sutherland, *English Satire* (Cambridge: Cambridge University Press, 1958), p. 38.

5. Ll. 1–14, in *Poems on Affairs of State*, gen. ed. George deF. Lord, 7 vols. (New Haven: Yale University Press, 1963–75), vol. 2, ed. Elias F. Mengel, Jr., pp. 205–8.

6. Ll. 25–34, ibid., pp. 200–4.

7. See especially *A Panegyric* (1681), ibid., pp. 242–45.

8. *The Word "Irony" and its Context, 1500–1755* (Durham, N.C.: Duke University Press, 1961), p. 24.

9. *Of Dramatic Poesy and other Critical Essays*, ed. George Watson, 2 vols. (London: J. M. Dent & Sons, 1962), 2:125–27.

10. *Augustan Satire* (Oxford: The Clarendon Press, 1952), p. 50.

11. *Verses on the Death of Dr. Swift*, ll. 57–58, in *Swift's Poems*, ed. Harold Williams, 3 vols. (2nd ed.; Oxford: The Clarendon Press, 1958), 2:555.

12. "The Ironic Tradition in Augustan Prose from Swift to Johnson," in *Restoration and Augustan Prose* (Los Angeles: William Andrews Clark Memorial Library, 1956), pp. 21–22.

13. See especially Maximillian E. Novak, "Defoe's *Shortest Way with the Dissenters*: Hoax, Parody, Paradox, Fiction, Irony, and Satire," *Modern Language Quarterly* 27(1966):402–17.

14. Knox, *The Word "Irony" and Its Context*, p. 24.

15. David Worcester, *The Art of Satire* (Cambridge, Mass.: Harvard University Press, 1940), pp. 90–108.

16. Quoted in Knox, *The Word "Irony" and Its Context*, p. 172.

17. *The Candidate*, l. 117.

18. *The Jacobite's Journal and Related Writings*, ed. W. B. Coley (Oxford: The Clarendon Press, 1974), p. 211.

19. See *The Ghost*, bk. 2, ll. 161–68 and note (p. 489); *An Epistle to William Hogarth*, ll. 633–34; and *The Candidate*, ll. 141–43 and note (p. 543), in *The Poetical Works of Charles Churchill*, ed. Douglas Grant (Oxford: The Clarendon Press, 1956).

20. Henry Craik, *The Life of Jonathan Swift* (London, 1894), 2:165n., as quoted in Knox, *The Word "Irony" and Its Context*, p. 173.

21. *A Discourse concerning the Original and Progress of Satire*, in *Of Dramatic Poesy*, ed. Watson, 2:115.

22. "The Muse of Satire," *Yale Review* 41(1951–52):82.

23. *Of Dramatic Poesy*, ed. Watson, 2:116.

24. On this matter of "enervate" critics see again the essay by Morris Golden, "Sterility and Eminence in the Poetry of Charles Churchill," *Journal of English and Germanic Philology* 66(1967):333–46.

25. See *The Poetical Works of Charles Churchill*, ed. Grant, p. 515.

26. *In Defense of Reason* (New York: Meridian Books, 1947), p. 140.

27. In "The Stretching of Augustan Satire: Charles Churchill's 'Dedication'

to Warburton," *Journal of English and Germanic Philology* 72 (1973) :360–77.

28. The original occasion of this was Hogarth's satirical print, issued in 1763, showing Churchill as an immense, club-toting bear. See *Hogarth's Graphic Works*, ed. Ronald Paulson, 2 vols. (New Haven: Yale University Press, 1965), 1:257–59.

29. Ll. 353–58, in *The Baviad and Maeviad* (London, 1797), pp. 58–59.

30. For a summary of the reception of the *Baviad*, see Roy B. Clark, *William Gifford* (New York: Columbia University Press, 1930), pp. 51–53.

31. *The Baviad*, ll. 309–17, in *The Baviad and Maeviad* (London, 1797), pp. 52–53.

32. *The Pursuits of Literature, A Satirical Poem in Four Dialogues, with Notes* (14th ed.; London, 1808), dial. 2, ll. 169–72.

33. *The Poetical Works of the Late Christopher Anstey, Esq.*, ed. John Anstey (London, 1808), pp. 75–76.

34. *Monthly Review* 48 (1773) :314.

35. *Satirical Poems Published Anonymously by William Mason with Notes by Horace Walpole*, ed. Paget Toynbee (Oxford: The Clarendon Press, 1926), p. 109.

36. *The Works of Peter Pindar, Esq.*, 5 vols. (London, 1812), 1:324.

37. Ibid., 2:381–82.

38. Ibid., 2:388.

39. Ibid., 1:82.

## CHAPTER 6

1. Preface to *Love of Fame, the Universal Passion*, in *The Poetical Works of Edward Young*, ed. J. Mitford, 2 vols. ("Aldine edition"; London, 1858), 2:55.

2. See for example James Sutherland, *A Preface to Eighteenth Century Poetry* (Oxford: The Clarendon Press, 1948), pp. 64–66.

3. *Spectator*, no. 1 (1 March 1711).

4. *Tatler*, no. 242 (26 October 1710).

5. *Epistle to a Young Friend* (1786), ll. 9–12, 49–56.

6. *The Progress of Error* (1782), ll. 9–12.

7. *Tirocinium: or, A Review of Schools* (1785), ll. 807–13.

8. For example, Swift's *On Poetry: A Rapsody*, or Pope's *Epistle to Augustus*.

9. *The Works of John Hall-Stevenson, Esq.*, 3 vols. (London, 1795), 1: 85–99.

10. *The New Foundling Hospital for Wit*, 6 vols. (London, 1784), 4: 142–43.

11. *The Conference* (1763), ll. 150–52.

12. *The Citizen of the World*, Letter 84, in *Collected Works of Oliver Goldsmith*, ed. Arthur Friedman, 5 vols. (Oxford: The Clarendon Press, 1966), 2:344.

13. He aspires to be "Poet of the People" in the "Ode to Irony," one of the

pieces included in *Odes of Importance* (1792), and flatly calls himself that in the "Ode to Jurymen" in *Liberty's Last Squeak* (1795). The allusion to his "friend" the public is in his note on the title of *Frogmore Fete*, which was published with *Hair Powder* (1795).

14. "Appendix: Containing the Author's Conversation with His Bookseller, &c.," in *The Poetical Works of the Late Christopher Anstey, Esq.*, ed. John Anstey (London, 1808), pp. 106, 117.

15. *The Works of the Right Honourable John Hookham Frere*, ed. W. E. Frere, 3 vols. (2nd ed.; London, 1874), 2:7.

## CHAPTER 7

1. "Essay, Supplementary to the Preface [to the *Lyrical Ballads*]" (1815), in *Literary Criticism of William Wordsworth*, ed. Paul M. Zall (Lincoln, Neb.: University of Nebraska Press, 1966), p. 174.

2. Opinion recorded ca. 1836, in *Letters of the Wordsworth Family*, ed. William Knight, 3 vols. (Boston: Ginn & Co., 1907), 3:122.

3. *Essay on the Genius and Writings of Pope* (4th ed., 1782), in *Eighteenth-Century Critical Essays*, ed. Scott Elledge, 2 vols. (Ithaca, N.Y.: Cornell University Press, 1961), 2:717.

4. Ibid., 2:762.

5. *Lives of the English Poets*, ed. G. Birkbeck Hill, 3 vols. (Oxford: The Clarendon Press, 1905), 3:251.

6. *Specimens of the Later British Poets* (London, 1807), p. xxix.

7. "Some Observations upon an Article in *Blackwood's Magazine*" (1820), in *The Works of Lord Byron: Letters and Journals*, ed. R. E. Prothero, 6 vols. (London: John Murray, 1900), 4:484–93.

8. "Notes on Selden's Table Talk," in *The Complete Works of Samuel Taylor Coleridge*, ed. W. G. T. Shedd, 7 vols. (New York: Harper & Bros., 1884), 4:379.

9. *Lectures on the English Poets* (1818–19), in *The Complete Works of William Hazlitt*, ed. P. P. Howe, 21 vols. (London: J. M. Dent & Sons, 1930–34), 5:69.

10. On this last point see Ronald Paulson, *Satire and the Novel in Eighteenth Century England* (New Haven, Conn.: Yale University Press, 1967).

11. Preface to the *Fables* (1700), in *Of Dramatic Poesy and other Critical Essays*, ed. George Watson, 2 vols. (London: J. M. Dent & Sons, 1962), 2:272.

12. K. G. Hamilton argues convincingly that such is the case: see *John Dryden and the Poetry of Statement* (East Lansing, Mich.: Michigan State University Press, 1969).

13. Reprinted as Augustan Reprint Society publication no. 2 (Los Angeles: William Andrews Clark Memorial Library, 1947), p. 5.

14. Robert Lowth, *Lectures on the Sacred Poetry of the Hebrews* (trans. 1787), Lecture 14, in *Eighteenth-Century Critical Essays*, ed. Elledge, 2:689.

15. *The Loves of the Plants* (1789), Interlude 1, in *Eighteenth-Century Critical Essays*, ed. Elledge, 2:1006.

16. As quoted in Alexander Chalmers, "The Life of Blacklock," in *Minor English Poets, 1660–1780*, ed. David P. French, 10 vols. (New York: Arno, 1967), 7:560.

17. *The Rebell Scot* (1643), ll. 27–28, in *The Poems of John Cleveland*, ed. Brian Morris and Eleanor Withington (Oxford: The Clarendon Press, 1967), p. 29.

18. *Epilogue to the Satires*, Dialogue 2, ll. 14–15.

19. *The Task*, bk. 2, ll. 315–21.

20. Ll. 15–16, 25–28. Text from *Poetry of the Anti-Jacobin*, ed. L. Rice-Oxley (Oxford: Basil Blackwell, 1924).

21. *The Works of Peter Pindar, Esq.*, 5 vols. (London, 1812), 3:388.

22. Ll. 17–24, 44–48, in *The Complete Poetical Works of Percy Bysshe Shelley*, ed. Thomas Hutchinson (London: Oxford University Press, 1934), p. 626.

23. *The Prophecy of Famine*, ll. 89–90.

24. See for example *A Century of Parody and Imitation*, ed. Walter Jerrold and R. M. Leonard (London: Humphrey Milford, 1913).

25. This was followed by a *Second Tour* (1820) and a *Third* (1821).

# Index

Addison, Joseph: on satire, 36–37; "Pleasures of Imagination" series, 75; mentioned, 11, 154. *See also* *Spectator*; Steele, Richard

Anstey, Christopher: self-portrayal, 64–66; *New Bath Guide*, 15, 64–65, 113, 144–45, 162–63; *The Patriot*, 65–66, 145

*Anti-Jacobin*, 4, 69, 70–71, 112, 157, 180. *See also* Canning, George; Frere, J. H.; Gifford, William

Armstrong, John: *A Day*, 15

Arnold, Matthew, 171

Auden, W. H., 167

Blacklock, Thomas, 174

Bowles, William Lisle, 170

Burke, Edmund: on visual power of words, 75, 76; *Enquiry into the Sublime and Beautiful*, 75

Burns, Robert: *Address to the Unco Guid*, 92–93, 159; *Epistle to a Young Friend*, 157; *The Holy Fair*, 92, 110, 178; *Holy Willie's Prayer*, 114, 116; *Reply to a Trimming Epistle*, 159–60; mentioned, 162

Byron, George Gordon, Baron: and subject of satire, 23–24; digressions, 31–32; self-portrayal, 72; and personification, 93; as ironist, 148–50, 174; styles of address, 163–66; on Pope, 170; *Beppo*, 31, 93, 148, 177; *Childe Harold*, 165; *Don Juan*, 24, 25, 31, 71–72, 89, 93, 118, 149, 159, 163–64, 179; *English Bards and Scotch Reviewers*, 23–24, 71, 143–44, 164–65, 180; *Vision of Judgment*, 149, 180

Cambridge, Richard Owen: *The Scribleriad*, 102, 108–9, 150–51; mentioned, 61

Campbell, Roy, 167

Canning, George: *New Morality* (with J. H. Frere), 70–71, 90–92, 112, 176; *The Friend of Humanity and the Knife-grinder* (with J. H. Frere), 180. *See also* *Anti-Jacobin*; Frere, J. H.; Gifford, William

Catcott, Alexander: attacked by Chatterton, 16–17

Cawthorn, James: *The Vanity of Human Enjoyments*, 12

Chatterton, Thomas, *The Consuliad*, 17, 88; *The Defence*, 90; *Epistle to the Reverend Mr. Catcott*, 16–17; *Kew Gardens*, 17, 29, 64, 88; *The Whore of Babylon*, 17–18; "Will," 18; mentioned, 14, 112, 142, 162

Chaucer, Geoffrey: portrayal of the Pardoner, 105–6

Churchill, Charles: self-portrayal, 19–